BLONDES IN BUSINESS

Audra Lamoon and Sue Gilkes

Blondes in Business

First published in 2009 by

Ecademy Press
6, Woodland Rise, Penryn, Cornwall, UK. TR10 8QD
info@ecademy-press.com
www.ecademy-press.com

Printed and Bound by; Lightning Source in the UK and USA
Set in Calibri and Bliss by Charlotte Mouncey
Printed on acid-free paper from managed forests. This book is
printed on demand, so no copies will be remaindered or pulped.

ISBN 978-1-905823-60-4

The right of Audra Lamoon and Sue Gilkes to be identified as the
author of this work has been asserted in accordance with sections
77 and 78 of the Copyright Designs and Patents Act 1988.
A CIP catalogue record for this book is available from the British
Library.

Acknowledgements

To all of our wonderful trainers – without you being fantastically amazing at what you do, we could never have done what we've done – thank you, thank you, thank you.

Thank you to Terry Cole, who supported us through all our journeys from day one.

Steve Edge, who branded us time and time again for free!!!

Raj Matharu....thank you for your generosity and friendship, we really, really appreciate you in many ways!

Jayne Rafter, who supported us in Cannes and in raising our profile with the RLI Mix!

Tom Miles, who supported us in Dubai till we got on our feet, bless ya poppet!

Rachel Walton, whose networking skills got us into all the right people in Dubai, even Bollywood!!!

Thanks to our book reviewers: Jo Seven, Phillip Benton, Anita Webster, Kelly Davis, Richard Norris, Jo Simpson, Janine Croft and Sue Simmons – great feedback, thank you for your honesty, you are all on our Christmas card list, and for Christmas….. you'll all get a free copy of Blondes in Business, hooray!!!

To Mindy Gibbins-Klein – Our very own book midwife – we would never have delivered if it wasn't for you – thank you for being a nag!

And a BIG thank you to Jason Dodd Photography who managed to make us look presentable – no mean feat! http://www.jasondoddphotography.com/

Dedications

Dedications from Sue:

To my three amazing kids, who are the only ones I can be truly myself around. I would never have been able to do any of this without you.

You have been my driving force, my believers, my inspiration, my dog walkers, housekeepers and my sanity. You have no idea how much I love you all and how proud I am of you.

To my Mum and Dad, thank you for your love, support, patience and the platform to spring from!

To My Brother – for being the one and only consistent man in my life!

To Kelly, Kiira and Helen for being true friends who have stuck by me, believed in me, told me to write a book and have been my memory, and thanks for the 'stories'. I promise to paint your eyebrows in our retirement home by the sea.

To all of the dogs that have been with me, thank you for your ability to love me whatever and making me get some fresh air.

John and Mel – without you both standing beside me both sides of the world and rescuing me in times of trouble, I may not even be here today – thank you from the bottom of my heart.

And to all the men I've loved before...............except one! Well actually two!! LOL - You know who you are!

And last but not least – Audra – I would never have done this without you nor would I of wanted to – you are my shining star as you know – I love you.

Dedications from Audra:

For my wonderful Mom Melonie, who has gone through so much in her life to give us so much, my mad brother Cy (who looks like Jesus) and sister Lisa Marie of whom I'm so proud. Thank you for being my family, small but perfectly formed!!! Not sure you know what I do really but hey you can read the book and find out!

For my precious pooch Coco and all the pets I've saved and yet to save.....!

For my god children Ellie and Grace, this may not be of any use to you now, but just you wait!

For Pops, although gone, I feel you around me in the most important times of my life, love you.

For Sue, get well soon, you have always been in my life and whether I see you a lot or a little, you always make a difference.

For Elaine's brother, Edward Thomas Knighton......who should have written a book on his life, you're always being celebrated, God bless.

To all my true friends who stood by me through thick and thin.... you know who you are!!!! I'm truly blessed! Cookie, Molly, Jof,

Michelle, Haydn and Andora, Mary (Step Mom to my pooch!) and 'Rowena the Repeater'.......where would all my funny stories come from if you weren't in my life? I love you all for standing by me through thick and thin...

And Sue...well...blimey, were we meant to meet or what? I love you like a sister and treat you like a Mom....its fab and I love you too!

From both of us

We really could go on and on and on and on – as you probably know! But suffice to say, to all that have touched out lives, we thank you, because what we have experienced is what has made us who we are today and if you had a part to play in that, we really do thank you and dedicate this book to you.

Oh and just one more...for Oprah Winfrey! We are sending you the book and if you read it then thank you, if you need us then give us a call!!!

Now we're welling up – so signing off!

Contents

THE UNSKIPPABLE INTRODUCTION

Skip it at your peril!

READ THIS – IT'S IMPORTANT!

Hey you! Listen! Sorry to be so bossy as soon as you open this book, but you will see in just one minute why we did! Now we have your attention...

Let's start again, friendlier! "Hi and welcome, how are you? On the brink of an exciting chapter in your life, we hope!"
So why did we want to write this book and why did you buy it? Well, we can answer the first question and only you can answer the second! We sincerely hope it provides you with what you want and need, but perhaps it won't be in the way you are expecting!

So let's get straight to it. No time like the present!

Boring old books! We have read several books and you may agree that you have to wade through the introduction, then several chapters of why, what, when, blah, blah, blah, BORING! So we, as you will come to realise, are slightly different people and we are certainly ladies of action - no rudeness intended, that comes later! But as Audra has the attention span of a goldfish (a successful goldfish), we thought of people like her when we wrote this, people who need us to get right to the point or at least tell a funny story along the way.

How to use this book whether you're a goldfish or a bookworm

1. If you just want an action plan for setting up your own business, steps to take etc., go to the chapter, Lights, Camera, Action! and pass on reading the stories if you dare – just get on with it.

2. If you know what to do yet have never had the courage to do it, go to the chapter on Fear. There is no shame in fear!

3. If you want to know more about us and where we come from, literally and experience-wise, then go to the chapter on Our Backgrounds.

4. If you want to hear about cock-ups we made along the way go to the chapter on Ups and Downs.

5. If you want a list of templates to use, business plans, time management, action plans etc., then go to the chapter, Lights, Camera, Action!.

6. If you want to know our personal gossip, well we have shared some it with you and popped in a few stories along the way when relevant - the rest can be shared with you over several bottles of wine at a fancy restaurant on your tab! Just check our diaries with us and we'll be there.

Write a book? Why don't yer?

Virtually all our friends have always said we should write a book; in fact some friends had even named it 'Never a dull moment'. A trip on a train is never just a trip on a train; there is normally a story to go with it, and we have dared to share a few in this book. We wanted to share our story of how, why and what we have done, because many people have asked us exactly that.

Men can play too!

There wasn't anything that we found that gave us a roadmap to setting up a business with the truth about what was entailed. There wasn't anything that we could relate to. Maybe it's because we are blonde!

We thought that this book might hit the spot for women in particular and different types of women in different situations. However, as always, never to be shunned, men you are more than welcome to read and use this book; you never know, you may well get some insight into how women think – now that would be a real gift! Particularly if you are a blond man! And if you also have blue eyes, please call us!

So if you haven't whizzed on to the Action Chapters and want to read this book in the traditional way, let's get started. Thought you might want to know a little about us and our situations. As we are about to share some time together, grab a coffee and, if it's after 5 p.m., grab a glass of wine!

OUR BACKGROUNDS

Bond, no sorry, Blonde Girls!

How we got here – Your past does not equal your future!

One of the most common things said to us in terms of running a business is **"I would love to do that, but I don't know how, what would I do?"** We sometimes feel that because we are female and blonde, people are particularly intrigued and what they actually are asking is "How did YOU manage to do it?" There are also assumptions that we have used our womanly wiles to get here, and of course we have! Why wouldn't we?

Ask any business woman and she will tell you that she has the following items in her wardrobe:

- The 'closing the deal' suit – low top, short skirt, smart and sexy!

- The 'meeting a woman' suit – trousers and shirt done up to the neck!

- The 'first meeting' outfit – gently does it, giving a hint of what could be!

We are all interested in how others have achieved what they have and, like most people, are always fascinated how people have got from A to B, which is probably the reason programmes such as *Dragons' Den* are so popular: we have all had brilliant ideas, haven't we?

What we don't understand is that if you are going to go on *Dragons' Den* then surely you would have watched a few programmes first and have realised that most people fail through lack of presentation, detail etc? Yet most contestants still don't make sure that they at least get these things prepared. And when they say they want the money for their salaries, well it constantly gobsmacks us as well as the Dragons! Sue has a goal to be invited on *Dragons' Den*, she'd love to give some of the contestants a piece of her mind! Audra is happy to settle for *Oprah*.

The difference between those who do have their business and those who don't is simple: some people have done something with their ideas and some haven't. We thought that it might be useful to put a chapter in the book about our story, and we sincerely hope that it just shows how two blondes with normal backgrounds have come this far and to assure you that **if we can do it anyone can!**

Audra's story

A Kent girl born and bred (town of Deal) I attended secondary school, which I despised and left as soon as I could to go to the good old US of A! To get my ticket money I spent a season on Hoverspeed, which is a Hovercraft service from Dover to Calais and Boulogne. I worked as cabin crew and I duly threw up on every rough day we had and, being the English Channel, that was most days! The passengers ended up looking after me a lot of the time so there came a point when I could no longer fly, yes we flew! We flew 8" above the sea so had Civil Aviation Authority training just like normal air crew. Eventually, I had to ground myself due to my unprofessional throwing-up episodes and, by chance, I was asked to train the next influx of trainees as all of the trainers had gone down with flu. Yippee!

Where it all began

The training Hovercraft proudly sat on the sea, on the harbour wall and I threw myself into it, not off it! Well, talk about baptism by fire, I'd only been there a season myself but I loved it and realised that training was for me and there started my life-long love of training and development. The CEO had called me in on a number of misdemeanours (I dared not to wear my scarf, hat and gloves in public!) but after the training sessions he told me I had done very well and should make that my career. Oh my God, what had he created?

However, America was still calling and I had to get that out of my system, so away I went and grabbed all the experience I could, starting off as a nanny to three kids under four. This may explain why I don't have children now! I also became an English confidante to the family... but that's another story! So I eventually returned to the UK on holiday to attend my Mum and Step- dad's wedding and ending up staying in the UK - like a stupid girl I stayed for a man, which eventually ended, naturally!

I returned to the ferry industry and worked as a ground hostess this time, as the sea was not for me and, as part of my role, I designed a training manual which we nicknamed the Hostess Bible and I was then 'borrowed' from one ferry company to another, the training side of me just shone through with each role I accepted.

Ferries, marriage and redundancy!

Eventually I was promoted to Port Manager's Assistant and even learned how to load a ferry (I was the first female at the port to do that, I'll have you know!) but I missed the training and contact with people and gladly took redundancy when offered, as the port was to close down…but just before it did, I met my husband to be (happily divorced now, thank you!) That 18-month nightmare ended with me renting out my house and looking for work in London or even abroad after spending a few years at Pfizer UK Ltd. I had a great job there with a great boss who actually became one of the main influencers in my career and life and a wonderful friend.

Debbie Cook was her name - boss and best friend - and she encouraged me to grow and spread my wings after my horrendous marriage ended, which coincided with my father dying of a rare lung cancer and my Mum totally falling apart and moving to Barbados, she just couldn't cope with the fall-out from Pop's death. At the time of Mum moving to Barbados, I didn't realise then just how important Barbados would become to me outside of great holidays, but this is where Sue and I met through Mum, so am forever grateful for that.

To top my non-fairytale life at this point, my nana was an alcoholic and getting worse by the year and my brother just disappeared (don't worry, he came back!) so I was alone at the ripe old age of 30 and I was single. However, I had the sending-off party of a lifetime and went to London to make my fortune, leaving death, divorce and sunny Deal behind me.

War zone!

So I'm now at a time where I am divorced, slimmer (good old stress) and raring to go and get a great job as a project coordinator in a well-known London architectural practice on the King's Road; all I could think about was the shopping! I didn't know what 'project coordinator' meant really but it was because they couldn't think of a proper title, but it didn't include training and at that time I soaked up experiences like a sponge. My first project was in Zagreb, during the Croatian and Bosnian war, helping to coordinate the new design of a pharmaceutical laboratory. I actually flew out there with the team during the war and we were sneaked slowly across the border when things got tough until we could return to work as normal. There were scary things happening all around and we were in a very precarious position; we were spat at and had money taken off us when crossing the border and that was by the immigration officers! Believe me it was very frightening. I managed to chalk that up to experience and moved on, country and employment wise - I wanted to train people, the urge was coming back!

I was eventually poached by a huge, top five Quantity Surveyors and Project Management consultancy in London and I became a consultant over a period of time, re-branding a department, recruiting and developing people in Risk Management training, not before I had to learn it all myself which I hated, I'm far too fluffy and not logical at all!

New York, New York

Luckily a great project came up in New York (ah, my beloved America!) and I jumped at the chance! We were looking at partners in New York and so had a series of meetings but mostly had fun. I must tell you the story of how I forgot to book the reservation at the Windows on the World restaurant in the Trade

Centre Tower. We were to take the clients for dinner and when I called to make the last- minute booking, they told me "Sorry, no room and a three month waiting list."

Frightened of telling my boss this, I wondered what he would do, so I called them back with a plummy accent confirming the reservation for Lord & Lady Beaverbrook and guests, at which they trotted off, mumbled something in the background and returned saying "Of course Madam, we have the best table for you and look forward to seeing you." Now, they obviously thought we were royalty and who was I to destroy their excitement? I didn't tell my boss or clients a thing and I had a friend join me for the weekend too, who witnessed the whole thing and panicked right up till we left for dinner in the limo!

We arrived all dressed up and a beautiful table was laid out, cordoned off by ropes (royal blue, very appropriate) and a row of very polished, well-presented waiters and waitresses, right up to the magnificent table that had a wonderful view of the Hudson River and Statue of Liberty, which looked like tiny specks way below us!

The Maitre D' himself took care of us and the clients were most impressed, but wondered why random people kept taking quick snap-shots of us! Even though I told the restaurant not to let anyone know we were coming and had specifically asked for 'no photos please'! Seriously! Free cosmopolitan cocktails flowed, it was the very first time I had tried one and fell in love with them instantly and drink them to this day! I could go on about how I stopped Lord Beaverbrook ordering Aberdeen Angus as we had a back-yard full of the beasts and how each time we got up the staff formed a bowing and curtsying line for us to the loo, and how we were announced on the dance floor followed by clapping, but I won't! The clients couldn't believe their eyes and actually thanked us for a brilliant night! My boss in turn rewarded me with NOT being sacked! Still, moving on... Oh yes, before I forget, I must tell you, we won the project while in New York, they thought we were fabulous. Naturally, the Blonde does it again!

The jump!

I had wonderful and not so wonderful experiences in my seven years of corporate life in London and eventually, thanks to a lady called Jessica Pryce-Jones, I jumped from corporate life to running my own business, the best thing I ever did! Then in 2006, Sue and I merged and Your Impact was born and we became an LLP in 2008 and we also launched Kawader Impact to add to our portfolio, which is our sister People Development Company, based in Dubai.

I always knew I'd amount to something, convinced I'd be a film star if I'm honest, but never got to stage school even though I begged my parents - they couldn't afford it and had ideas of going to New Zealand, so stage school was out of the question. I used to stay with friends in London who were actors in *Grange Hill,* the children's programme about a London school and the Green Cross Code adverts among other things, and I was in love with the idea that I could be a child star too!

I thought they must earn millions but their careers took another form, one became a dustman and the other enjoys her career at Debenhams, so not all actors make it big! So my acting skills, such as they were, came alive in my training career.

Like most people, I've had incredible lows and incredible highs in my life. I've been without a penny and relatively well-off, but being happy in my work and having a stable home is key for me and I trust in the universe, Mother Goddess and divine intervention at all times. I believe everything happens for a reason, there are no coincidences and if you don't learn lessons the first time around, the lessons will keep on coming until you do learn them, believe me! So any lessons you need to learn to stop them happening again? They are quite easy to spot, does the same thing keep happening to you? Does life seem to throw the same problems at you? Umm, it might well be you need to look into dealing with it differently next time! Over to Sue...

Sue's story

I, like many people, wanted to have my own business and I didn't know what to do and, to be honest, I fell into every business I have ever had, purely by chance; it wasn't planned, it wasn't due to some amazing talent. An opportunity came along and I took it. What I have learnt through my business experiments, though, is that you will be successful if you enjoy what you are doing, you believe in it and you have the personality traits for it. So my recommendation to you is to ask yourself two very simple questions: What were you naturally good at as a child and what do you do with your spare time because you want to? And don't say 'What spare time!?' And don't say 'Washing and cleaning!' What do you do just because you enjoy it? Whatever it is, I bet you are good at it!

Reading is a passion of mine and I love to learn from books. The other great passion of mine is learning; learning something new, not that you would know it when playing *Trivial Pursuit*! My school reports always said throughout my entire school life 'Susan is easily distracted' but whose report didn't say that? It must be part of the teachers' training! I think the reason is simple, we can't be interested in everything and anything we are taught, not every subject engages us, so my question to you is 'What engages you now and what engaged you when you were younger?' Maybe you need to ask someone in case you have forgotten!

The early years

I was an early reader and from an early age I would read to the class at story time; I read all the books in the school library, I would walk down the stairs in the morning reading, I would even cross the road reading! (Don't try this at home!) One of my earliest memories was children laughing at a book I was reading, or was it me? I was goofy and Mum and Dad made me wear school uniform when nobody else did, plus my surname was Pratt, how unlucky can a girl get? Anyway back to the story. The book I was reading was called *The Bastard King* by Jean Plaidy – it was a historical novel and I was about eight, but kids being kids we thought the title very rude and therefore hysterical rather than historical, while I just read whatever I could get my hands on, and would read whatever my Mum was reading.

I guess my story of school life is fairly standard, did okay, not brilliantly, I was a bit rebellious in the earlier years, ran away a couple of times and even shamefully kicked a teacher! Due to my parents' work, I moved schools and homes a fair bit, three times in my first year at senior school, so I don't have very fond memories of school really. I left at 16 having had a conversation with my careers officer, I said that I wanted to work in a nursery; he took that to mean I wanted to work with kids, what I meant was I wanted to work outdoors at Bristol Zoo Gardens! Anyway my parents thought that I would be good working with kids, so I took the exam to get into Clifton Nursery Nurses' College. I passed and that was it. I actually have a lot to thank the misunderstanding of the careers officer, because that was my introduction to learning - learning through play, lesson plans and classroom control - all very useful to this very day!

The teens...

I couldn't wait to leave home, no disrespect to my parents, but I wanted to travel, have fun, stay out past 9 p.m. and explore and becoming a Nanny seemed the ideal job to achieve these not so professional objectives. So I got a job in London - four kids and a Jewish family, I had to do all the cleaning, cooking and look after the kids and I was only 18! But I did have my own room and bathroom and £40 each week all to myself, heaven! What an experience that was. I could tell you so many stories but not today, we'll do that over coffee someday.

I'm sure you don't want to hear my whole life story, so I'll whizz on! I didn't go travelling; I came back to Bristol, married my childhood sweetheart at 19 and worked as a Nursery Nurse in a brand-new nursery for Avon County Council. It was a wonderful time, but a time when we seriously lacked cash! So we needed more money, we had our first child, Kate, and money was tight and we weren't sensible with what we did have, who is at 21?!

First stab at running a business

So we started looking for part-time work, evening work. I worked in a pub; that was hard work and smelly and damp, I only lasted a short while! Then I worked at a Wimpy burger bar running children's parties on a Saturday, and then we came across an advert, you know the ones 'Earn £500 a week part-time'. Well, that was tempting considering I was on £4,500 a year! We went to a meeting, it was a multi-level marketing company called L'arome selling copycat perfumes. I know, I know…. but guess what? It was the making of me, I met my first ever mentor and I learnt to sell, I learnt to be positive, persistent and I learnt to train and found that I had a flair for it. We did really well, ended up doing it full-time, earning £3,000 a month back in the 90s and going to America. It was fab, but the bubble burst and the company went kaput and we both had to find full-time jobs again and by then we had our second child, Rebekah.

Taste of corporate life

Fortunately one of the ladies we had met during our time with L'arome was now working at Yellow Pages and recommended me to them and I landed the job selling advertising space over the telephone. I wasn't there long, as I then had my third and final child, Samuel, but the training that I had there was outstanding, they were renowned for it. When I went back to work, Sam was just four months old, money was still tight, and I got a job with an IT training company because of my Yellow Pages training, and the directors were also ex-Yellow Pages. When I look back it really is incredible how each step along the way led to a better and more positive stage!

I developed a lot during my time at this company, went from Telesales to Account Director for what was then British Rail and learnt a great deal about training and what makes people tick, most importantly what made me tick; it wasn't the money, which was lucky, as my first pay cheque with this company bounced! What I loved was learning, and I believed in what we were doing as a company; the MD was such a visionary and took time out to spend with me and, of course, for any young person this was highly motivational and it kept me there for three years. To be honest, I only left because the company hadn't paid me for three months; sadly, motivation and learning didn't put food on the table. I was lucky enough to be headhunted by another training organisation and there began a whole new chapter of my life.

Sun, sea, surf and...

Not long into my job and after a serious illness, viral encephalitis, which is a swelling of the brain, I decided to leave my marriage. Now that I was single, a colleague at work asked me if I would go to Barbados on holiday with her as she was going alone and wanted some company. So to cut a VERY long story short, I went and met a Bajan man called Tony who, after three years of long-distance dating, I married in the UK. Not long after that I went with my Sales Director to a new company, selling and delivering e-learning, which was now the latest thing in training. I did really well there and made some fantastic friends and got promoted to Channel sales, which involved training other companies to sell our e-learning products as part of their portfolio of services. It was a great job, but very stressful, which contributed to my marriage breaking down, me never seeing the children and generally not being happy or well. Tony and I decided that if we moved to

Barbados, I could take a break, not work and I could get better and see my kids and it all sounded a perfect solution, so that is what we did. We decided in October 1999 and by January 2000 we were there!

I didn't work for seven months and BOY was I bored, so I started to work and I did loads of things I had never done before: I wrote e-books for a training company in the UK; I designed and set up websites; I started a book (didn't finish that one!); I worked for a scuba-diving company; I set up a holiday booking company - lots of bits of things. Then I was offered a job as HR and Training Manager with the hotel chain my husband worked for, and that was a challenge! I eventually realised that my service values were not in line with the chain's owner's money values, so I left.

I really wanted to get back into training, and I wanted to make a difference and I felt customer service was the way to go, so I partnered an IT training company and set up a business skills training side to their business and qualified as an instructor in Customer Service, Sales and Business etiquette. I also wrote two columns a week for the national newspaper *The Nation*; I was setting up and running events for the wealthy part-time and in general life was good, although my marriage was not. We eventually parted, amicably though (well, as amicably as any couple can!) and I rented a house near the beach and took in a friend as a lodger. Through my lodger I met Audra; she came home one day and said "I have just met Mel's daughter, Audra, you two would get on so well together and you do the same kind of stuff!" So we met and literally that was it!

Back to the chilly UK

We did some work together and Audra said "If you ever come back to the UK we must work together" and I said "I will never come back"! Oh how I learnt the lesson: Never say Never!

One year later I was back in the UK, arriving on December the 15th, bit of a shock to the system I can tell you! I can't say the reasons for our return here, suffice to say 'family issues', so I came back, got a job as a director of a HR and Training consultancy, purely to get a salary, which would give me my credit rating. Warning: if you leave the UK for more than three years, you have no credit rating on your return (maybe that's a good thing!). I bought a house and then I took the maddest leap ever, according to my family.

This is an excerpt out of my journal called 'Women of 40', Jan 01 2006.

I actually believe that the 40s are the new 30s, Christ I feel occasionally 17 and act it! My poor Dad came to see me today and found his 40 year old daughter face down, fully dressed, comatose on New Year's Day. He bought a cup of tea and didn't say a word, bless him. Last time I drink Portchini! (homemade potato wine for the uneducated! Don't ever try it!)

I often check my 18 year old to see if she is still breathing at 4am after one of her nights out, I guess it never changes, you're always the parent and we love our kids warts and all.

Anyway I digress, my journaling 'need' today is: LOUD DRUMS BEATING PLEASE. Thank you, pause, big breath, I am going to hand in my notice. I am going self-employed *and taking back control of my family and me. Down to us. And we will do it – in fact we've done it. So there. But boy am I s**ting myself! I get feelings of "Oh my God, this makes me feel odd or is it nerves or instinct, someone please tell me".*

It all sounds so good and right, the circumstances are healthy, much more than most when they start. And I am strong, brave and I can do it. I can win business, big business. I can motivate and manage a team. I can be organised, I can let go and delegate.

So I have all the skills and qualities I need, armed with a short skirt and the amazing ability to bullshit and oh of course, the blonde hair, I'm a winner.

Now onto the subject of men, whom I meet a lot of through work. I am a new woman. Getting to know someone, kissing, sex only if in love – Ha! I will not fall in love on the first night either. So no escape, treasure and pleasure yourself until Mr Right shows up.

The birth of Your Impact!

I got my mortgage in November and handed in my notice in January. Understandably, my family were concerned, but I wanted to work for myself again, I loved it, so off I went! I set up Your Impact and worked closely with Audra's company Lamoon Business Solutions (LBS). We were doing so much together at that time that it seemed ridiculous for us both to have separate companies when we knew that together we could not only make it work, but we would be unstoppable!

And that is the story. I am still amazed at how life has turned out and I feel that this is the beginning now of a whole new chapter. The universe has so conspired in every conceivable way to bring us to this point that it really excites us. You may not believe in the universe, God, or whatever but, regardless of what you believe, we are 100% positive that every opportunity is there for the taking, if you look hard enough and are trusting enough to take the leap. If it is the right decision, every step will be supported and made simple.

So let's get back to you

Blimey, don't we go on? So what do you want to do and why? Now look for the opportunity to move your ideas forward and if they are with good intention, you will be shown the way.

Tips and food for thought

- What were you naturally good at as a child?

- What do you do with your spare time because you want to?

- If you were guaranteed NOT to fail, what would you do?

- If you are holding back, why? Think seriously and be honest with yourself

- What has your past given you: lessons learnt, experience for example, that will help you right now?

FEAR

Fear? What Fear? Blondes aren't easily scared!

Fear, it's just a four-letter word!

And Audra knows lots more four letter words, but getting back to Fear.....we have had our moments of sheer panic! So we felt that we needed to write something about fear, because for anyone wanting either to start their own business or just do something they have never done before, there is likely to be an element of fear. We would like to say up front that this is from our personal point of view; we are not Dr Phil and have no certificates that qualify us to talk with you about fear, apart from our own beliefs and personal experiences of having to overcome it!

Dubai or not Dubai? That is the question!

So what advice do you choose to take? Well, if Audra had listened to all the negative advice she received about Dubai, regarding being a woman doing business in Dubai, then our Dubai Company, Kawader Impact! may never have existed. Sue had delivered some training for our clients there twice before, so she had a glimpse of what was acceptable, but we were told that we wouldn't get business because a) we were women and b) you guessed it, we were blonde!!!!!! Outrageous comments! Because in reality our being women and especially blonde has got us the attention we need to get us in front of people, along with hard networking of course.

So FEAR could have played a part if we had let it, but we decided that the people spouting the fears hadn't actually been or worked there and were just passing on hearsay. Mindy, our editor, asked us why we weren't fearful of going into Dubai and we were pretty stumped! It actually shows how much we believed in ourselves and it obviously wasn't pushing the boundaries of our delivery. To us it was just geography, as we had been delivering training globally anyway; it was just paying for a company, office and marketing that was in question and all the usual fears were dispelled when we talked it all through.

Learning the culture, however, was an obvious activity and we are still learning today, as their culture has agreeable and disagreeable sides, as with everywhere else. FEAR was not an option here, it was just a warning device to make sure we covered all the basics, so thank you FEAR!

Cultured blondes.....US?!!!

Yes, we had to work on this attribute we admit, but before going into any culture, country or business you have to do your research first and that's exactly what we did and what we do; remember, how else can you make an informed decision? The boom was apparent in Dubai and people were living a great lifestyle and opportunity was everywhere... BUT, we decided not to rush into it and to take time in gaining the right business partner, not one who was in it for a quick gain but someone who wanted a long-term company and who was part of it too. We wanted a business partner, not just a sponsor who legally has 51% of everything and doesn't have to work for it.

Meat to meet

Audra had many lunches, dinners, teas and coffees with potential partners, clients and associates. Audra rarely eats meat, so the lunches became a bit monotonous for her (poor old girl, eh?) and one particular day an associate introduced her to our business partner in Dubai, Dr Bassem Younes (as partners/sponsors have to be local and Arabic). It was another buffet lunch, meat everywhere! Audra, Steve (associate) and Dr Bassem Younes (potential partner at this time) all plated up and went to sit down when Audra spotted the chocolate fountain. Well, that was that, business lunch or no...Audra subtly dumped the stir-fry and ran for the fountain; the falling, velvety milk chocolate called to her, begged her to dip pink marshmallows into it and never leave its side....so Audra did her best! With that, Dr Bassem followed suit, got very excited by the sight of it and, in a demonstration of solidarity, dumped his stir-fry and grabbed a plate and they both loaded them up with goodies and drowned it all in chocolate. As far as Audra was concerned, he had shown all the qualities of becoming a partner right there! After several more meetings led by him and after more research and country visits on both sides, we decided he was right for us and he decided we were right for him. Dr Bassem had been looking to work with a training and development company for five years and until we came along simply hadn't met anyone who shared the same values and level of integrity and capability as we did at Your Impact!

We must stress here that having the **same values** is vital in business, not only with your business partner but with your employees, associates, clients (and lover girls!) - believe me, you will see why later in the book.

So with FEAR being heeded, advice and research undertaken and instinct acknowledged, we set about launching a Dubai company and office and the rest is history! Hence our constant tans!

What the scholars say

The Oxford English dictionary states that *fear is an unpleasant emotion caused by the threat of danger, pain, or harm or the likelihood of something unwelcome happening.* Well, that's interesting eh? Therefore it is not real! It is the prospect of something happening that you don't want to happen, but it hasn't happened – yippee!! And it actually might not happen – double yippee!! Fear is just script-writing negative events in our heads. So 'stop script-writing' is a mantra we often use or we'd never do anything!

Think back to when you learnt to drive, you were probably petrified at the beginning and now you probably don't even give it a second thought? Same kind of thing, eh?

Thanks a bunch for fear!

Flight or Fight? Which are you? In any research that you do on fear you will come across the 'flight or fight response' also known as the 'Fright, Flight and Fight response'. In simplistic terms (don't worry, we're not going to get all scientific!) but when we actually face the 'thing' that we have feared, the fear actually disappears and we react; our bodies now use the fear to produce adrenalin, so the fear goes away and is replaced and we either stand our ground or run away. Either way, we no longer feel fear, we do something! Okay that might be a bit scientific, but you get our drift.

So that really makes feeling fear a little pointless doesn't it? Or does it? Surely fear must have its benefits or why would our bodies have the ability to feel this way? The key benefits that we can see are:

a) It makes you think twice

b) It encourages you to prepare

c) It encourages you to research the alternatives

d) It makes you consider the risks versus the opportunities

Now, what is quite odd about that is that any good advisor would recommend that you consider the above four items before attempting a new venture, the same items that fear makes you feel so, in actual fact, fear is a GOOD thing, it's our internal voice telling us to consider our options before we take action because, let's be honest, when we are advised by anyone else to do the above four things, we are likely to yawn, rebel or just not bother!

Negatrons

Which brings us nicely to the next point: it is often the people closest to us that give us such advice and, of course, it is good advice as we have gathered, but it is often their voice of fear that is speaking!

• What if you make it – will that affect your relationship with them?

• What if you don't make it – will you be asking to live with them and borrow a fiver?

Just ask yourself some simple questions:

1. Have they ever done what you are about to do?

2. If so, did they make a success of it?

3. Are they qualified by life to advise you?

People are often so well-meaning, but do be aware of the negatrons. Have your negatron spray to hand, have on your suit of negatron-proof armour and prepare yourself for battle – because it is a battle you will have to face! But we say 'Bring it on!'

The best people to talk to are those who have no emotional ties with you, and the ones who have done it before and done it successfully. Go, seek and find – they are out there.

'I think I'm going to die, really!' Panic!

Drama, drama, drama! We certainly do not want to over-simplify fear or rather the feelings that fear gives you, because if you have ever suffered from anxiety, panic attacks or any related condition then you have our full sympathies, as we have both suffered to varying degrees. Sue at one point thought she would have to give up her job due to panic attacks; every time she got in the car, on particular motorways she would get an attack - not brilliant considering she was doing on average 30,000 miles a year! It took her six months to get over it and required her to shout at herself in the car "Come on then, give me the most massive attack you can, come on" and it actually worked!

What really helped was knowing why they happened. It also helped knowing that no-one had ever died of one! Huge relief!

Research and preparation for car journeys - sweets, coca-cola and cigarettes in the car - all helped massively. Hence why we felt that by getting fear down to its raw basics might be of use, hope we were right? We both have had to make BIG jumps, leaps of faith, some of the experiences we have shared in other chapters.

One of the most useful things in helping us in dealing with our fears we have found is reading. A couple of books that we have both read that you might find helpful are:

- *Fearless Living* by Rhonda Britten

- *Feel the Fear and Do It Anyway* by Dr Susan Jeffers

All the books we have recommended throughout this book will benefit when fighting the 'fear'.

So what are you afraid of anyway?

Okay, we have discussed the fear of failure, so what else are you afraid of?

Write them down, and then do this: pretend that your best friend came to you and said they wanted to do this and he/she shared the same fears, what would you say to them?

Write next to each item on your list of fears something positive that you can do to minimise the risk. Talk to a supportive person, a person with experience, not a negatron!

Example: Opening a Knickers factory! Pros and Cons...

Pros	Cons
Own business	Investment
Limitless earning potential	Lack of security
Lifetime supply of knickers!	Getting knickers in a twist!
Limitless success	Fear of failure
Improve lifestyle	Give up current lifestyle
Gains	What do I have to give up?
Be my own boss!	Scared of doing accounts
Work own hours	Lack of dependable salary
Perverts!!! Can always see benefits of both!	Perverts!
Lingerie launch party	When knickers become bloomers!
Male range, male models	Family/friends want freebie frillies!
I could be famous!	I could be arrested!! Not really, I just like freedom, some call it flashing!

What about this for a thought? **What would you do if you had no fear?**

Imagine it is a success; make a list of the differences it would make to your life.

Now that should get you excited! If it doesn't, maybe it's not worth bothering with then! Here are some of our reasons for jumping and becoming our own bosses:

Differences in our lives
Freedom
Time off
Time with family, kids, oneself
Creativity
Travel
Charity donations/work
Being at home
New friends/contacts
Money!
Fun
As many duvet days as you need!
Hangovers can be hidden!
Meet more men! Yippee!
Appreciation of life, family, pets and home
Can afford more rum and chocolate!

So what's the worst that could happen?

Okay, let's take it one step further: a great question to ask yourself is **'What is the worst that can happen?'**

This is a question that we often ask ourselves, it really helps to put some situations in perspective: "Could we cope with the worst happening, yes or no?" If it's yes, okay then let's do it. If it's no, then let's not do it, or at least can we do anything to minimise the risk of the worst happening? This is another book on its own; you really must acknowledge and accept your answer to that question before you go into business for yourself. Also, when established in business, there are risks of it failing and you have to ask yourself the same question in order to make a decision about whether to continue or wind up the company or simply start again. Once you accept that you could lose it all but can regain it, rebuild or start again, the fear lessens and the focus goes back on to succeeding. This is when Back Up Plans come into their own: better to be prepared than caught in the headlights.

Bastards or businessman – you decide!

Global contract calling! Let's give you an example: we landed the best contract ever, providing training around the world as a joint venture with another training company. The partnership up until then had been very successful. Then unfortunately the ownership of the partnership changed and boy, were we thrown a curve ball! Everything changed, nothing remained the same and we had no control whatsoever, all the contacts, shared values, processes and procedures and financial arrangements went out the window overnight and a 12-month battle ensued.

We were in the middle of running a global leadership training programme for them, which had been given rave reviews and expansion of the contract was imminent. However, we weren't being paid! We negotiated, we pleaded, we threatened and still no money! So we then had the massive dilemma of pulling out of the project and letting the end client down or continuing in the hope that we might get paid. We took the latter route for six months and still no money, so we had to pull out. The sleepless nights and constant phone calls and downtime were incredible. We were so angry, upset, hurt, disbelieving and shocked that the whole host of emotions played havoc with our lives and also actually made us irritable with each other, which is a total rarity, and we think that was when we decided enough was enough. We had to stop reacting emotionally and put our hard business heads on and hand it over to someone who knew what they were doing.

To cut a long story short, we had to go to court and we won!!!! Yippee. But it was a lesson learnt, as ever, in a tough way and has caused us to buy extra-strength face cream to erase the wrinkles and hair dye to hide the grey! Thinking of buying shares in L'Oreal **Lesson here – Feel the fear and do it anyway – thank you Dr Jeffers!**

So let's say you are thinking of setting up a business, what are you afraid of?
Let's make a wild guess and say it's fear of failure. Okay so let's say you failed.
Now what? What would you do? Could you go back to doing what you do now?
The answer is probably yes to the last question.

So if that is the case – you would be no worse off, just more experienced!

Oh yes, of course, we mustn't forget this fear, the shame and embarrassment of failing - is that the real fear? Be honest, come on, be really honest! Hand on heart and all that! Brownie's promise – dib dob dib!

That fear is completely understandable, but you know what? The people that really care about you and the people you should have in your life will rally round to help and the people that you think might taunt and laugh behind your back, well you don't want them in your life anyway, do you? Sounds like something Mum would say!

How many times have you experienced or heard people say "Due to this experience, I have found out who my true friends are"? Loads of times we are sure.

We wouldn't recommend that you put your house up for collateral and there are many ways you can run a business without putting your home and family at risk. Borrow someone else's money for a start! Go on *Dragons' Den.* Why not try out your idea part-time in your spare time? Why not get some skills at evening class first? Go into partnership, pray for redundancy with a massive payout!

As the saying goes 'Where there's a will, there's a way'! How much do you want this? Enough or a 'nice to have'? You need to decide that, but don't let 'fear of failure' stop you, that is just pointless!

So regardless of fear, living your life as you want it to be has to be a good start. Fear does not diminish with time, age or experience. Fear will get you each time you want to move on, grow, diversify, change jobs, move house, get married, take on employees, get rid of employees! Working in different countries and cultures, all scary!

An acronym we had learnt, not sure where it came from, sums this all up really nicely:

FEAR – False – Evidence – Appearing - Real

So stop script-writing and do it anyway!!!

Suggestions and thoughts that might help:

- Feel the fear and use it

- Consider the risks versus the opportunities

- Speak to people who have succeeded, preferably in the field you want to go into

- Get support, get a coach or mentor

- Get a large can of Negatron spray and shares in L'Oreal!

And for God's sake – if it all feels and looks right – bloody do it!

SIGNIFICANT PEOPLE

It's their fault!

Significant people – it's all their fault.

Have you had anyone influence you enough that you wanted to change? Our husbands were originally those people, but moving on to positive influences!

There have been, are, and will always be people in and out of our lives with lessons attached to them for us to learn. We are both strong believers in that whatever the lessons, good or bad, you need to learn them OR they will be constantly repeated, they will reappear and heavily disguised!

We need lessons to know what NOT to do just as we need to learn what TO do, and so the lessons go on. We believe they will be always be significant and in this chapter we wish to share a mixture of both with you.

We do hope that you can learn from them, and use them for your success as well as avoid some pain!

Who on earth was brave enough to influence us?

Our significant people are many and equally diverse; however we've both limited them to two people who have made an impact on our personal as well as our business lives and to whom we can attribute who we are now and where we are now.

To be honest we could never ever, not for one single moment, list all the people who have made an impact. Parents, children (to whom Sue attributes her sanity - at which point Audra shouts "Are you bloody mad – keeping you sane?" - and to keeping her feet on the ground!) Friends, business associates, lovers, husbands, chance encounters, colleagues and dogs! We thank you all and apologise for not giving you a personal mention, but where would we possibly start? Are we forgiven? Good – so let's get on with it then! Audra first...

Audra's first significant person

Debbie Cook, or 'Cookie' to Audra to differentiate her from her other friends called Debbie! Cookie was Audra's boss when she joined Pfizer in the Training Department. They got on famously and she offered Audra a role in Facilities Management under Cookie's supervision, which Audra jumped at as the training she was doing had become more IT training management which wasn't the training Audra wanted to do, partly because she is IT phobic but mainly, to be honest, because she just has no interest in it!

Cookie was a calm, focussed, driven woman whose career rose from being a cleaner, to inputting data to a Facilities Management Manager to European Manager to being even more successful today.

Audra learnt many qualities from Cookie such as: always see both sides of any story, dispute or problem; do the job properly; get it right by asking questions; and always be fair and honest.

That's not to say that they didn't have fun because FUN is the one thing they always had. Audra has some outrageous stories that we could tell you but then we would have to kill you, or we can tell you in another book using false names! However, we can let you in on some of the antics that were not too damning!

There was one occasion when Audra had to drag Cookie from under her desk by her ankle to meet a supplier that she just couldn't stand! Her instincts were right about him, though, and he was released from a preferred suppliers list due to an indiscretion!

Audra used to use the company credit card to give the receptionist teams coffee and Otis Spunkmeyer biscuits every day. We'll let you make your own jokes up about the cookie name!

One day, Cookie pretended the bill was HUGE and called Audra into the office to tell her off then fell about laughing! It was meant to be a weekly treat that had got rather out of hand and become a daily routine. "It was for team-building purposes," Audra insisted. Of course, it had nothing to do with Audra being a chocoholic! The moral here is not to get too familiar with your boss's generosity or credit card!

Audra has endless stories about their practical jokes on one another, in fact they joined up as an incredible force to play tricks on others too...especially with a new and difficult manager who tried to break the great system they had in order to make a name for herself; let's just say Cookie and Audra got their own back!

Singing Nuns

One of the funniest stories we can share was when they dressed up as singing nuns for a company commercial; Audra wrote the song, it was called 'We Are The Vision Missionaries' and they performed it dressed as nuns in the company studios where it was filmed. It went around the world and at employee motivation events such as the Winter Gardens in Margate. Yippee, world fame at last! However, after filming they managed to hang on to their costumes and ran amuck on site and even blessed a truck driver or two passing through! Security was alerted and by then they had all guessed it was Cookie and Audra, not to anyone's great surprise! So many more stories to tell but we think it's only fair to wait until Cookie retires! Audra still has the unedited video, which sends her into hysterics even now! But it demonstrates that they had fun as well as working hard. Audra and Cookie always gave their best, and were often acknowledged for it so that gave them more fuel and leeway to have more fun of course! Fun is a constant theme in our training courses, as we believe people learn more through being relaxed and able to laugh.

And, we all have email stories to tell don't we?

Audra wrote an email to a very 'conversationally-challenged' person; in this email she said he was 'boring her to death' and she also said she'd seen garden slugs get more out of life than him… and then promptly sent it to him by mistake! It was meant to be forwarded to Cookie, not replied to the originator. So Cookie had to pull out all the stops to get Audra out of that one! The moral there being never reply to an email if you want to vent …start a new one, DO NOT put a name in it, then you can write what you like and delete it, and at least it's out of your system but not out in the world!

But seriously…Audra learnt a lot from Cookie. She also learnt a not so good technique from another previous manager at a London firm, which taught her how to bluff and showed her where bravado can get you. His name we'll not mention here as he also had stalker tendencies, which scared the life out of Audra. Still, we can take the good from any bad situation can't we?

The good the bad and the ugly...we're not talking about three blondes!

Talking of taking the good from bad, Audra had a supposed friend/advisor who guided her professionally in the very beginning and proofread literature, gave advice etc. However, it soon became very evident, although not soon enough, that he was an emotional wreck who bled poison into their friendship and that of her friends. The lesson here is be careful who you trust, you must research your advisors, don't trust or believe in just anyone. Pay for advice if you have to. Audra didn't, and she let the relationship encroach into her private life, a major lesson that cost her initially but made her stronger and has made her stand for no nonsense ever since. What doesn't kill you makes you stronger, they say, and how right that is!

This is what Cookie had to say about Audra:

"I first met Audra when she applied for a temporary role working for me in the training centre. On the very first introduction I knew there was something about this girl that was special.

We just hit it off both professionally and personally and the great thing was we were able to keep the two separate. Audra has been in my life and the life of my family life ever since.

I think she played on the blonde bit at times but I knew that underneath there was an extremely intelligent person, or should I say 'responsible person'!! 'Responsible person' became a bit of a joke as she was referred to in this term during an induction for new contractors working on site. 'Should you have any problems contact the responsible person in your area, Audra Lamoon'. At that time, 'responsible' and 'Audra' were not words you would use in the same sentence.

I was in a position to be able to give her a variety of roles and soon moved her from the receptionist role; she had more in her than that. Plus, I needed to get her away from the office PA system. During a busy lunch and a high-profile management site visit, Audra thought it a good time to test the new PA system. I was sat in my office and the ding dong start of the message sound come across, then Audra's voice ... "this is a test call, this is a test call". But the actual message sounded like "this is a testicle, this is a testicle", and soon you could hear mutterings and laughter and me running to reception to shut her up. Audra being Audra she got away with it, though, through her charm and approachable attitude.

She became my right hand girl in FM and was able to take on almost anything I asked her to do. I knew she would go far and I am absolutely proud of what she has achieved. Audra has had some tough times and been let down quite badly by people in her life and this had really dented her confidence. I wanted to help her and coach her back into believing in herself and using her natural skills to go on and do bigger and better things. As they say, the rest is history, we do very different jobs now, but I am still in her life and always will be. When she is down I remind her of her achievements and how she has overcome a lot to get to where she is."

Debbie Cook

Head of Application Change and Support, BUSINESS TECHNOLOGY, Worldwide Technology

Thanks Cookie, the cheque is in the post!

Audra's second significant person

Audra will always thank Jessica Pryce-Jones (cousin to Helena Bonham Carter - just had to get that claim to fame in) for pushing her into getting her own business! Jess came to interview at Audra's company (London Project Management Company) to become one of their training providers when she was a consultant. Although Audra had delivered a lot of training, this was a different standard altogether back then, she is more than happy to admit that! It was also industry specific, so Audra was in complete admiration of her. Jess's interview to be a trainer was with Audra's boss, who was more interested in telling Jess all about himself rather than hearing all about Jess! What a weird interview that was, not sure he even heard what Jess sounded like!

Audra eventually moved on to another company, and she and Jess maintained contact. Audra knew she wanted to run her own business at some point and Jess was the perfect person to learn from. They were meant to meet! Jess, a fellow blonde (so one of the gang!) invited Audra to attend as many training sessions as she could and asked her to join in and help out as much as possible too, till one day, two years after meeting, Jess told Audra in no uncertain terms to get off her ass and run the training herself and that she should start up her own training company.

Audra didn't have the belief in herself that Jess had in her at that time, but the conversation stayed with her and Audra studied Jess hard, which stood her in good stead. Audra even took leave so she could observe Jess with other clients, corporate levels and different industry sectors, such as banking, for example. Then Audra made her decision and couldn't wait to jump. By then she had considered all that she would have to give up; a posh London flat, flash car, BUPA and a super salary but, despite all the perks, she had no time to enjoy it. She was really scared at this point but she read 'Feel the fear and do it anyway', which made her focus on the gains and not the losses.

Equation

Therefore Audra's personal, burning dilemma was:

Fab salary+ benefits in undesirable location *versus* uncertain salary, no benefits in desirable location

So, the trade-off was giving it all up in London and going back to the sunny Kent countryside living in her 17th century cottage with her pet cat Puddles, and doing what she liked, where she loved! Decision made!

Here's what Jess has to say about Audra:

> *"I first met Audra at a job interview. She was sitting in on one of the craziest job interviews I've ever done. The person who was supposed to be interviewing me did all the talking*

– so much so that I set myself the task of seeing if I could make him talk even more. Something we both achieved. But halfway through the interview, I caught Audra's eye and she winked at me conspiratorially. At the end of my lopsided conversation, I was told that it had gone 'exceptionally well' as I was escorted to the lift. "See you soon lovey," Audra told me. And although I knew that I couldn't work there I wanted to get to know Audra more. Her cheeky wink had set her apart in my mind. Sure enough she called me up soon after and told me that she wanted to set up her own business and wanted some mentoring and support to get there. I knew at once she could do it: she had the drive, determination and sense of humour that would help her succeed. So I was delighted to say yes. I soon discovered that she had common sense in buckets and an irrepressible attitude to everyone and everything. And so I embarked on one of the funniest working relationships I've enjoyed so far."

Jessica Pryce-Jones

Managing Director, IOpener

Sue's significant people

Sue's two people are ones that have had more of an impact on her mindset. Like Audra, Sue is a strong believer in how you think is what determines the outcomes you get; in fact, one of our company sayings is: *'If you do what you've always done – you will get what you've always got'* There are many sayings that have the same meaning: 'What you reap is what you sow' and so on and so forth! Sometimes those sayings really piss you off, eh?

Sue met her first significant person in her twenties; he was the first person she had ever encountered who talked about 'positive thinking' and he completely opened her eyes to a whole new way of life and way of thinking.

Up to this point she had no idea or understanding of how thoughts could determine actions which, in turn, would produce results. It sounded mad! But now it sounds mad to even think that there was a time when she had no concept of that, but we don't know what we don't know, do we?

He was a family man who had his own business, which Sue became involved in. It was a business that relied heavily on a positive mental attitude and the ability to convince others that a positive mental attitude was a must – not an easy task!

Sue, once her eyes were opened, read and devoured all that she could find on this new way of thinking; some books she would recommend anyone to read are:

- *The Power of Positive Thinking* by Norman Vincent Peale

- *The Power of your Subconscious Mind* by Joseph Murphy

- *Unlimited Power* by Anthony Robbins

All of these are available from the website –
www.blondesinbusiness.com/books

There is a host of books on the subject and these books are pretty old in the grand scheme of things, but they are brilliant and had a big impact on Sue.

Sue also believes that surrounding yourself with positive people is of major importance, you need to be told you can do it, you need to be told it's possible and you need to believe that what they see in you is true. Flattery only works for some of the time, as nice as it is! But genuine belief in you and support and mentoring is invaluable. We all look at some people and wonder how on earth they have achieved what they have, and yet the answer is simple: they believed that they could do it. Why on earth would you attempt to climb Mount Everest, for example, if you believed you would fail?

Okay that might all sound a bit trite and of course people have doubts, but if you didn't have doubts you probably would fail anyway as you wouldn't prepare thoroughly, you would be blasé and complacent, which are all ingredients for disaster.

Positive thinking got Sue a house - really!

In fact, positive thinking and believing in the power of the subconscious gave Sue her current home. The story goes like this. When Sue came back from Barbados, she rented a house but actually thought buying would be better and more grown up although, obviously, there were pros and cons.

If she bought a house she wouldn't be throwing £700 a month in rent down the drain - a pro; she wouldn't be able to up sticks and move abroad again – a con. BUT also a pro as she needed (or so she believed) to be settled. But maybe that was a con as 'settled' was not a word Sue was completely comfortable with because it made her feel old!

But if she was settled then so would her children be, which would be a pro; they could finish school and Sue couldn't just wake up one day and decide to move as she has been known to do! One of the great things about getting older (not old).... is that you get to know yourself and put obstacles in your own way (to manipulate situations, hee hee) if needed!

Anyway the theory was all very good, buying a house would be a good thing but for one small and quite important fact: she had no money; no deposit, no solicitors' fees and no money for all the other little incidental costs that buying a house seems to bring.

So she took a leap of faith, and did as the book said; dutifully wrote out her positive affirmations, stuck them to her bedside cabinet and read them every night and every morning, just like the book told her to. You might laugh, and so did her parents when they stayed over and she had forgotten to rip them off her bedside cabinet and hide them to avoid the teasing that Sue knew would ensue.

So with no money and not a hope in hell of the positive affirmation 'I live in the perfect home for me and the kids', three months later Sue and her children were in a five-bedroom house just down the road! Yep, honestly they were.

Sues second significant person

Sue's is overjoyed with the fact that her second significant person, Gay Taaffe, is still in her life. Gay lived in Barbados and they were introduced through Sue's friend Alicia. In preparation for this book, Sue asked Gay if she could remember their first meeting as

Sue couldn't, and Gay can't either; she wrote in an email – 'all I remember is much laughter'.

Gay ran a couple of businesses in Barbados, including Bomba's, a fab beach bar on the west coast. Wouldn't be surprised if that's how Sue and Gay met! Anyway Gay was, and still is, a very spiritual lady who lived in an amazing plantation house called Chimborazo in the parish of St. Joseph. Gay had the fantastic idea of turning it into a place where like-minded people could meet and learn more about spirituality and run workshops. Alas, Sue was not a like-minded person but, despite this, Gay was still friends with her and Sue ended up, sceptically and begrudgingly, attending one of these weird workshops, which was on meditation, run by a well-known lady in the spirituality field called Sue Minns. Our Sue took to it immediately which she herself was surprised at, not being one for sitting still for long, let alone being quiet!

Sue did disrupt one such workshop as she forgot to turn off her mobile, which rang very loudly, yet the rummaging in the handbag to find it seemed much louder! Then it beeped saying there was a message. Sue was very embarrassed and then got the giggles – not what you want to happen during a group meditation!

Gay introduced Sue to so many aspects of getting to know yourself, the power of the universe and, in particular, meditation which Sue will tell you saved her life, guided her through making tough decisions, gave her peace, and a whole host of other things. What was truly amazing was that Sue then started to share this with others and ran meditations on the beach, and even the beach guys joined in without a spliff and liked it! Holidaymakers began to join in and shared their experiences. It was so powerful and to this day Sue will always thank Gay for providing the opportunity to be given such a wonderful tool, to be given the friendship and openness and honesty and support during a time when Sue was very much in need of it. Today Gay is still a major influence on Sue's spiritual journey.

What Gay had to say about Sue

"I don't remember how Sue and I first met, but I do remember a bright sunny person who brought a great energy into the room and was always positive. Sue was always, and still is, a fun-loving, humorous, energetic girl who laughed and cried at the same time.

Always ready to lend a hand and offer encouragement despite being busy herself and she was courageous enough to start a meditation group on the beach at sunset and to bring challenging people into that circle and she kept that circle going instead of giving up.

Sue is someone who has the ability to mix and socialise with all types of people: non-judgemental, open-hearted and always acting with the best of intentions."

Gay Taaffe

Oh those good intentions! That has been a tough one to live with, not everyone has always agreed with the actions that have been made with good intention! It's hard being misunderstood! Sue wishes to put in at this point that while she was writing this, despite her love of meditation and Gay's kind words, she feels a bit of a fake as she was sat in bed smoking a cigarette, with her dogs under the covers snoring! So please don't think for one minute that she is all religious and pious, she is fairly normal and just happens to like meditation – hey, why not have a go, you might just like it too – and you don't have to wear a kaftan or sit cross-legged on an itchy mat, however inviting that may sound!

Things for you to think about….

- Who are your significant people?

- What do others see as your strengths?

- What do you think about? Do you think positively?

- How have negative encounters affected you?

- How strong are you in standing up to negativity?

- How do you want people to remember their encounter with you?

There is a simple tool to help you with these kinds of questions, go to: **www.blondesinbusiness.com/significantpeople.html** and download a free questionnaire.

SPIRITUALITY

No chanting please,
we're serious!

My God! What do blondes have in common with spirituality – is it a brand of hair dye?

Why on earth do we have this chapter? Well, we believe most of us have something that we use that is not part of the physical world yet we listen to it, rely on it and relate to it. We all have a different name for it; we see it, feel it and use it in different ways.

Or you might not believe in anything or you might believe in one or two of the following:

God	Witchcraft – white or black
Allah	Buddhism
Jehovah	The Universe
The Virgin Mary	Superstition – if I don't walk on the cracks of the pavement, I'll have a great day!
Jesus	
The Holy Sprit	
Angels	Old wives' tales
Demons	Intuition
The Devil	Self-belief
Prophets	Something is out there but I don't know what!
Saints	
Mother Goddess	Religion

The list goes on and on… but we two blondes personally believe in a higher self that wants us to succeed, learn and help others, and we try to embody that in all that we do. We are passionate about people, education, training, animals, children and welfare so we work towards helping people and animals as much as we can, and the universe, Mother Goddess and God all help us to achieve these goals because we believe we can do it and help ourselves. Here endeth the lesson!

Bondage! Now that we have your attention…

Why 'Religion' as an item on the list? Surely if you believe in a God you are religious? Well, we are not church-going folk but there is a lot of debate about the origin of the word religion and there is a lot of disagreement about whose religion is right! But generally the dictionaries trace the word back to an old Latin word religio meaning 'taboo, restraint'.

A deeper study discovers the word comes from the two words *re* and *ligare*. *Re* is a prefix meaning 'return', and *ligare* means 'to bind'; in other words, 'return to bondage'. Okay, we are happy with that!

The list above is fairly long but could probably go on and on, and each one of us is more than likely to say that they have believed in an item on the list at some point in their lives. We have turned to it, taken part in it, believed in it to get us through various times, particularly when times are hard. Have you ever promised God that you will give up drinking if you get through this hangover? We need the help of a power greater than ourselves sometimes, if not all the time. Would you agree? Yes we know there are atheists too; we would be keen to learn what or who they turn to.

Masturbation causes blindness!

An outrageous thing to say, but we've all heard it (or was it just Sue who was taught that?) The old wives' tales and the superstitions could be a volume of books, not a paragraph in this book, but here some of the ones we have come across in our lifetimes:

- Don't wash clothes on New Year's Day or you will wash all your luck away for that year.

- An itching foot means a journey to somewhere new.

- Shiver and your grave is being walked over (very odd considering we're alive!).

- Put a sixpence in the bath of someone who is ill, add herbs, then dispose of the water in the middle of a crossroads, to throw away the illness.

- Don't eat yellow snow – Oh no, sorry, not an old wives' tale but it is a wise one to follow!

Joking aside, although we don't take superstitions and old wives' tales seriously, spirituality plays a huge part in our lives. For example, Mother Goddess came on holiday with us! Let us share...

Big Mark the miracle!

Well, we say miracle but really it was revenge! Audra had been disappointed by a male 'friend' and so suggested we pray to Mother Goddess to get her own back, just for a laugh and not to hurt anyone, but to test her sense of humour...we proceeded to pray at the same time out aloud, hands clenched together, elbows resting on the bar and eyes closed (what must we have looked like?) and said almost word for word that we wanted a big, muscled, good-looking man to come along and pick Audra up and make a fuss of her...in front of the soon-to-be ex male friend! Amen!

Within 45 seconds this massive man appeared and made a fuss of us and Audra said to him that she had bet that the next man to appear would lift her up! He took the bait and the bet and lifted her high above his head...he was tall, massive and strong and just loved us Blondies! He did it again and again... it was hilarious and the desired effect took place, making the soon-to-be ex very aware, jealous and available!!! We must add there is no business link or moral to this story, but the ladies reading this should love it and know that Mother Goddess can appear very quickly and with a fabulous sense of humour! Try it... read the book *Mother God* by Sylvia Browne, she will teach you how to ask for things in life.

Spirituality - What it's not, in our eyes!

Well it's not hell and damnation if you don't believe in the 'Right God' that's for sure and apart from that we know as much as you do – that is why it's called a faith, it is something you cannot guarantee and prove (although some say they can), so you have to have faith, trust and belief.

What is it then?

So what is spirituality and its relevance to this book? The relevance bit is an easy question to answer, while 'What is spirituality?' is a little harder, but we both believe in the power of a force greater than ourselves. We believe we have proof; what others might consider coincidences we believe are events that happened through a divine intervention, they were meant to be, for good or bad, because there are lessons that had to be learnt to help us grow, develop and move forward.

We are sure any theologian is spitting feathers and screaming 'What simple-minded idiots! What blondes!' Yes we are, but it works for us, it gives us hope, comfort, exciting adventures, giggles and trust. as we do believe that if our intentions are good, then the pathway will be made smoother and easier to ride and obstacles will disappear. In summary, our definition of spirituality is being in contact with a higher self. Not an easy thing to define, never really tried to define it before, and it may be a very over-simplistic view, but considering no-one knows for sure and no-one can convince us all to believe in the same thing, it can't be wrong, even if it can't be guaranteed, right?

The benefits of belief

Having the belief that we are on the right path and that everything is happening perfectly gives us comfort and relief and allows us to go forward with our decisions and actions when we both agree on a subject, way forward or task. Then we are happy, regardless of whether it turns out to be the wrong move or not because we know we will still learn from it and move on. That comfort stops us from deliberating for too long, we make decisions and act very quickly and we have learned that this is a good quality for us both to have. We both believed in setting up a business in Dubai, and becoming a LLP in the UK and in hiring and releasing employees etc; and they were all the right decisions, feelings and actions for that time.

Mother Goddess

Mother who? You may ask, we only learned about her in 2008 and can't tell you how many times we have called upon her for help... yes us, two normal (relatively), professional, capable modern women, talking to Mother Goddess! Please read the book *Mother God* by Sylvia Browne... even if you don't believe you should be moved and what have you got to lose?

We talk to her a lot, we even write letters to her. In fact this very New Year (2009) we sat at the most northern point of Barbados and opened a letter to her that we wrote a year before. We had sealed it and kept it to read one year later to see what came true. It was a success, we had achieved about 90% and you can attribute that to Mother God or hard work or just by writing it down. Most successful people write down their goals so it's a good habit to form even if you don't believe in it...statistically you will achieve them! So you can talk to her, pray and write but believing in her is key, for us.

Just as we write down our personal and professional goals, we take her seriously and believe we will succeed - and we will!

Intuition

Most people have it, and women have incredible intuition in bucket-loads, so use it! We have intuitive thoughts about people we meet and situations we find ourselves in and instinctively know if it's a good or bad thing, right? Then trust it and go with it. We have times when we both think the same thought at the same time, share it with each other and then make a decision based on that and no other evidence...and it turns out to be right.

Deliver the dollars!

Must tell you that we are working in Bahrain (delivering Customer Services to an airline) where the culture is completely different from ours. Blondes are respected there and they can't believe the stereotype we have in the UK... yes, we are goddesses in parts of the world! Or maybe not, you've seen our pictures!!

But you see it pays to research because now, as a result, we are focussing some of our business efforts in Bahrain and that came out of the client looking for a suitable company to provide customer care on the Trainer Base website!

Let us tell you it was a risk because the client wanted us out there at three day's notice, after one telephone call! We had no way of knowing who they were and how trustworthy they were, but they offered to pay for flights and hotels in advance, which was a good sign! But, in reality, we did not know if they would honour our fees etc. and a lot of hard design work had gone into the workbooks which were to be used, but we both thought it felt right.

The lesson here is there's always an exception to the rule and that's because instinct or intuition told you to go for it. Ahh intuition, there it is again, use it and see what opportunities it can bring!

Tips!

- Acknowledge your beliefs and use them daily

- Coincidences! They are not coincidences, it was meant to happen! Embrace them!

- Trust your instincts

UPS AND DOWNS

We like these, a lot!

Ups and Downs, or whatever you want to call them!

Ups and downs, ecstasy, cock-ups, excitement, and massive blunders! We all have them! Some days are just worse than others, for whatever reason - maybe whenever the moon is in opposition to the sun!

We had one of those days when things didn't go according to plan! Audra and Sue were meeting up in London for a couple of appointments; the morning started with Sue not being able to find a pair of tights without a ladder, ending up with her having to cut one leg off two pairs to make one ladder-less pair! Little trick for you! Always buy the same tights and then you can use this little gem! Men, you may find that useful too!

Sue had loads to prepare for her two days in London: pack, print handouts, feed dogs, but unfortunately they didn't get a walk! Dropped her daughter off at the shops and went to the train station. Of course, as you know, when you are in a rush to get somewhere, all the bloody Sunday drivers are out on a Thursday morning for some strange reason and, of course, a slightly wet road causes major delays, also for some unknown reason!

Sue got to the station but the car park fairy had deserted her (probably because of the rain!) and she ended up parking illegally, again! So she went to the ticket desk and told them (because she got fined last time), bit of a recurring problem for her!

Bless the ticket office, they told her a colleague of theirs was leaving, told her where the colleague was parked so off Sue went thinking 'that is good customer service!'

She didn't mind by this point as her 11.02 a.m. train had been cancelled!

So she parked legally and was now in plenty of time to catch the next train. Got her ticket and a complaints form about lack of parking! And off she went to the waiting area. Now Sue travels this route a lot, about twice a week, she keeps trying to persuade Audra that a London apartment would be a good idea but Audra won't have it!

When you travel a route a lot you get to see the same faces and now Sue had some time on her hands she had a quick chat with the little Welsh ticket man, which is when he asked her out for a drink! Now Sue is not size-ist or racist because a) it would be hypocritical to be size-ist as size 12 has always been elusive, let alone a size zero! and b) she is married to a very black man! She's dated short and tall men before but never a Welsh man, only because the opportunity had never really presented itself, unless you consider that meeting a Welsh man on a train who wanted to massage her feet and had a self-confessed foot fetish to be an opportunity! Sue turned that one down as she did the train ticket man, politely, and disappeared as fast as she could!

So Sue sat down and texted Audra her little interlude to keep Audra amused on her train journey. Then Sue's name was called out over the tannoy system - and very oddly they pronounced it correctly, so she actually recognised it! She had a horrid momentary thought that it was the ticket barrier man but she was told to come downstairs to the information desk where she had left her credit card in the machine! It really was one of those days wasn't it? Or is it the hair colour? And it was only 11.20 a.m.! So then she had to walk past the ticket barrier man again! Sue tried to look busy fiddling with her phone and just smiled briefly and sat down.

Failure – what's that?

Really and truly, without being hyper-positive, annoying bubbly blondes, we really do believe that there is always a lesson that needs to be learnt and if you take one precious gem of information away from the so-called 'failure' that stops you going through a 'failure' again, then you have had a success!

You're always going to have both successes and failures so accept that and move on... as we always say!

To be honest, when we have mucked up, it has occasionally caused sleepless nights, but over time we have learnt not to dwell on so-called failures or crises; we now diagnose the problems, see what could have been done and prevent them from happening again...then move on...yes move on!

Keeping a positive attitude is absolutely vital. We are both especially good at self-talk and we both help to lift each other if we are feeling low, disappointed or hacked off. It doesn't even have to be work-related, personal stuff does get in the way; to say it doesn't is just not true. While writing this book, we had a call booked with our coach Mindy when Sue had an email about one of her foster dogs, Rocky, saying that he had cancer. Sue had had Rocky for three months and he was one of her favourite foster dogs. He is an old Boxer, nine years old, huge and slow and so affectionate. He was found by the council while cleaning out a house from where the tenants had been evicted. He was found locked in a garden shed. When he first came to Sue, he had no voice, couldn't bark, probably from all the barking and crying from being locked up. Some people are just so wicked and cruel.

Sue was so upset to hear that Rocky was so ill that she called Audra to tell her and say she couldn't possibly do a coaching call; Audra started crying too but said that she would do it and pass on the information. The good news is that Rocky is responding well to treatment and is coming back for a two-week holiday while his new owners have their holiday! Can't wait to see him.

Rocky. Sue was more concerned that her bin was in the photo, please pretend you haven't noticed, and no Sue, we won't air brush it out!

This is when a partnership, whether business or support from friends and family, really comes into its own. We really do support one another and one is always stronger than the other when it counts - even if both of us are crying, one of us is crying less!

Relying on, trusting and understanding how each other operates and how that neatly fits into your ways is paramount in making a business partnership work. If only we could have applied those principles to our marriages!

We both absolutely know our own strengths and our lesser strengths... let's not call them weaknesses please! Pushing your strengths even further is key to success, don't waste time on what you can't do, and get better at what you can do!

There is a great book by Marcus Buckingham called *StrengthsFinder*, which advocates that we should focus on our strengths and be fantastic in our natural abilities. The book also gives you an access code to do an online test so you can find out your core strengths – try it out.

To trust or not to trust, that is the question?

We mentioned how we have been blessed with clients, trainers and associates. However we have been in a position where trainers have tried to approach our clients, and clients have tried to approach our trainers! This happened because we trusted people too much and assumed their values matched our own without putting in enough effort to check them out.

In our mind their actions are very short-sighted. Yes, you might get an extra client or piece of work, but that will be the last piece of work given by us and you should never bite the hand that feeds you!

Listen, just because you want to trust someone doesn't make them trustworthy.

So what did we do? Well, we set about designing a process to ensure the trainers and associates we met matched their criteria. On a practical level we get references and form a buddy system where we observe the trainers and they in turn observe us to see if the fit was right.

Honest and productive feedback is given both ways and at every stage. We discovered that if we deviated from this we could have problems but if we managed it properly there were none, or at least fewer!

Failing that, a good shout, scream and cry should get you in the mood to get rid of the buggers!

A quick history lesson...

We all experience failure and the aftermath. But how you cope with the failure is the important element. Often the peak of frustration comes right before a major breakthrough. That's if you don't quit. So don't quit!

Remember – Quitters never win and winners never quit!

Below are several success stories from history where failure was a frequent companion throughout these great people's lives. Let's all take some inspiration from their stories.

Abraham Lincoln

Failed in business in 1831. He was defeated for the legislature in 1832. He failed in business again in 1834. His beloved, Ann Rutledge, died in 1835. Had a nervous breakdown in 1836. Was defeated in election in 1838. Defeated for

Congress in 1843, 1846, and for a third time in 1848. Lincoln was defeated for Senate in 1855, and defeated for Vice President in 1856. In 1858 he was defeated for Senate. And finally in 1860 he was elected President!

Thomas Edison

Built 1800 prototypes until he created the first light bulb. He was one of America's most prolific inventors, and he was granted 1,093 patents by the U.S. Patent Office, including motion picture cameras, the phonograph, and the storage battery. But his inventions included such failures as a perpetual cigar, furniture made of cement, and a flying machine.

Alexander Graham Bell

Bell invented the telephone, and yet he found it difficult to secure a major backer. In the same year that he patented the telephone, 1876, Bell tried to sell exclusive rights to the telephone to Western Union, the leading communications company at the time, for $100,000. William Orton, Western Union's president, declined the offer, saying: "What use could this company make of an electrical toy?" The rest, as they say, is history.

Frank Herbert

Herbert is the author of Dune, the epic science-fiction tale. The book was rejected by 13 publishers with comments like 'too slow', 'confusing and irritating', 'too long', and 'issues too clear-cut and old fashioned'. But Herbert was persistent. Dune went on to win the two highest awards in the science-fiction writing and has sold over 10 million copies.

Albert Einstein

Einstein was a poor elementary school student. He failed his first college entrance exam at Zurich Polytechnic. However he went on to develop one of the greatest theories of Physics, *The Theory of Relativity*. He won the Nobel Prize in Physics and today his name is synonymous with the word 'Genius'. He will go down in history as one of the greatest scientists in the history of the world.

Henry Ford

Ford failed in business and went broke five times before he finally succeeded. In his first car, he forgot to put in a reverse gear. Then in 1957, he created what he bragged about being the 'car of the decade', the Edsel. This car was infamous for its doors that wouldn't close, a hood that wouldn't open, paint that peeled, a horn that stuck, and a notoriety that made resale impossible. Despite this, Ford went on to achieve much success.

Colonel Harland Sanders

Yes, the Kentucky Fried Chicken Guy. Before his original recipe made it to the big time the Colonel traveled across the country trying to franchise his business. On the 1009th try he got his first sale. Today, KFC is a worldwide success story.

These guys had incredible guts and belief, didn't they? Where are all the girl stories? In the absence of female stories – back to ours...

Case History – Position, position, position!!!!!!

We created a position for administration support at the start of 2008 as we were very busy and the admin side of things held us back from doing what we were good at.

However, we didn't research the salary properly or the job specification for what we actually needed and consequently we paid far too much for our company to be able to afford it, and so the position began to cripple us once the recession set in with the result we had to make a redundancy after 10 months.

What was the lesson? We should have researched the salary and managed the expectations we had of the person. We needed admin help, yes, but we needed a salesperson more. Even though we had combined the two we didn't ensure a sales process was in place or that the person was good at sales. We happily handed over the admin side of the job and ran off to network, deliver and design. In an ideal world that would have been great, but the role was not what the company really needed and there was no return on investment in hindsight. Ah, that wonderful thing called hindsight again!

So our advice to you when taking on staff is: research the actual role you really need for the business, not just to relieve you of tasks you don't like, because there will always be tasks you don't like!

Work out an acceptable salary that won't drain your resources some months down the line and recruit effectively, which does not necessarily mean hiring someone that you like. When running a small business it is critical that each person adds significant value.

We have redesigned our recruitment processes significantly through lessons learned and now they are part of our own recruitment training courses, which are fantastic even though we do say so ourselves! Nothing like learning by experience eh?!

The good thing is we recognised it early enough and made the correct decision in time, making the position redundant and reassigning admin duties to each other.

This released the capital needed for Audra to go to Dubai more and continue the great progress we had made with the business there. We launched the company in 2008 and so we needed to be there mainly to maintain growth, profile and relationship management. Even in a global recession, there are business needs and you have to be there to provide for them.

Tenders

We don't like tenders, and rarely go for them as they take a lot of time and we don't always win them. We could look at them as failures but we don't. Firstly we feel sorry for the client for making the wrong decision in not picking us and we always ask ourselves "What does it free us up to do that we couldn't if we'd won?" Besides, tender work is often not so well paid, so work out how best your time is spent in hours and costs versus wins.

However, understanding why you haven't won a contract is paramount and getting feedback from the client is crucial for future development. If we liked the client then we always try to keep in touch as it just meant that particular job wasn't for us at that time, and the next one might be!

If you lose on cost you have to re-visit that, naturally, but don't compromise on cost either because you should be charging what you are worth. Educated clients will always pay as long as there is a return on investment. You will see and hear that a lot. You have to be sure you can deliver your promise and understand the client before you start offering your services willy nilly. You can sell a rubbish service once but never twice! Besides, as you know, word of mouth marketing is very powerful especially when it's bad news!

Finishing on the Ups!

Successes can be measured in many ways; duplicating success is the key to sustainability. Success means different things to different people; what do you see as a success? You may measure success in terms of money, turnover or salary, projects won, time at home or time away. However you measure it, you need to enjoy it and prepare yourself for the future because you never know what is around the corner, life does like to throw you the occasional curve ball!

Bank not only the money but also the contacts and lessons learned throughout.

Can Do approach – that old cliché that works!

We Blondes do generally have a 'can do' approach to most things in life and even in a perceived crisis we have the ability to see beyond the implications of a trying time or crisis. Positive thinking enables us to go for it and going for it enabled us to open up our office in Dubai, right at the end of the golden years when everyone boasted about raking it in... then global recession hit Dubai as well as the rest of the world but we are still there, changing our strategy to fit the needs of the market. Flexibility is definitely a major part of being successful.

We invested heavily in the Dubai project for two years so looking after our new clients and understanding the market was important in staying put. We believe in speculating to accumulate and so the return on investment for Dubai remains to be seen.

Oi!

Audra also researched and then gained distribution rights for a Health and Safety gadget, (Oi Noise), which can be sold across the MINA region, (Middle East, India and North Africa) and in the recession this is another option for revenue. We always look for complementary services or products to make our service stronger and help the client to shop in one place. It's about giving a holistic service and helping others to gain business.... 'Givers Gain' remember? (We should charge BNI each time we quote their motto!)

Lots of ex-pats have left the Emirates as a result of the global recession but we have not! We will ride out the storm because we are good at what we do. It remains to be seen how successful we will be... we'll write another book and tell you of course but, for us, realising our dream of having a company in Dubai has already been achieved but that is just the start, we now have to maintain it, sustain it and grow it.

Networking has been as important in Dubai as anywhere else and we enjoy it too, so much so that when Sue is holding the fort in the UK and sees pictures of Audra tagged on Facebook, she wonders if networking is a cover-up word for partying!

How does success happen?

Well, not by chance, though seemingly lucky opportunities do come by and you must grab them when you can; however it seems **the harder you work the luckier you are!** Heard that before? Well, read that again and understand that it means you get lucky by being active, by putting in the effort, so it's not luck, it's success out of hard work, not luck.

We don't believe in coincidences, there is no such thing, but you do always need to be alert and ready for opportunities as they come along.

Keep doing what works, always be selling, always be marketing, always service your clients. It's important that you continually feed the pipeline of prospective business, both new and repeat business.

We have provided a simple tracking device on the website for you to use; for goodness sake do not leave it to your memory, you may not be blonde but you're also not a robot, there are too many things to keep track of so use all the tools you can!

Yes m'Lord!

Making quick but informed decisions has saved us from potential disasters. For example, remember that partnership that provided us with work all over the world? They stopped paying even though the client's feedback was excellent and with a little research, we found out why; they were pouring all their funds into another venture and we were not the only ones not being paid. It was a ploy to make their accounts look healthier than they were. It wasn't personal but equally it was not workable; the company values between our two parties were just not the same.

Over time we were owed in excess of £50,000 and so the training was pulled after several warnings and then we had to make a tough decision not to carry out any more work because what was the point? Sadly a court case ensued, which we won as you now know, hooray for blondes in business – don't mess with us!

We should have pulled the training before, we should not have left it so long, but the clients we were serving on behalf of the partnership were important to us and we really didn't want them to be affected. This was the only reason that the training was delivered for so long.

So now there are processes in place, lawyers engaged and terms and conditions revised. Sometimes you have to engage outside help for such things; it does cost, but the cost of not doing so can be a lot more considerable!

The good news is the clients we were serving on behalf of the partnership have come to us directly so, you see, good can come out of bad! Don't be too scared to make a tough decision and make a stand when you need to.

Maybe this might help you. It is an excerpt from Sue's journal.

> *"I can see a view of what is in front of me, there are hills and valleys, but the grass is so green and the sky so blue. I have an actual image in my head at this moment of writing. It is so exciting to know there is so much more and more to enjoy, to live and learn and the valleys are normally quite small eh? The hard bit I guess is the going down and the climbing up, but when I see it like this a whole new perspective opens up, because when you are coming down, you've just come from somewhere wonderful, so each time we can be grateful and excited and by feeling positive we will move faster through the valley and maybe the valley is a place of rest too. Thank you spirit for giving me this gift. I should share this insight and gift – give it to others. It makes you not want to have flat plains – how boring – no views, no interest, nowhere to head for. Thank you for my ups and downs".*

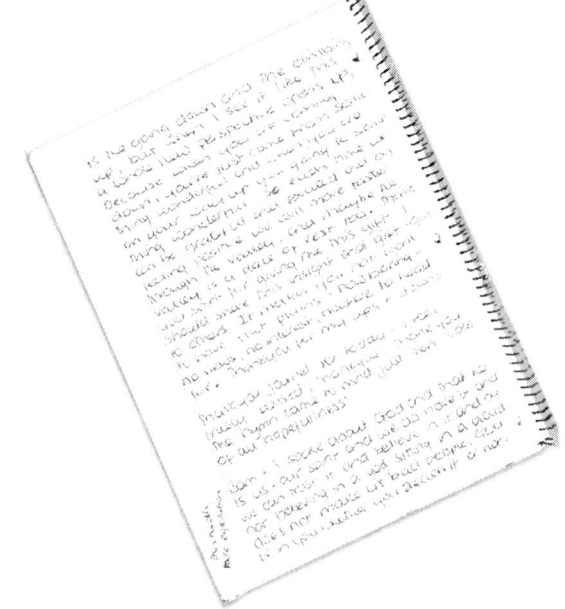

Phew! That was a heavy chapter, let's lighten up shall we? But before we do let's look at some tips, you'll thank us for them!

Tips!

- Be honest with yourself about a problem or challenge, find a solution or two and do it, don't delay

- Don't start something you can't finish

- Research your associates, advisers, banks, accountants... in fact anyone associated with your business

- Have insurances, policies and procedures in place to protect you and the client

- Don't rely on memory, use tools to help your business

- Keep doing what works – keep selling!

- Be positive even in frightening times, look for the good and look out the not so good, the bad and the ugly

- Duplicate success and surround yourself with successful people

- Put money aside in the good times, ready for the not so good because where there is a boom, there may follow a bust – recessions and booms are cyclic

NETWORKING

Some people confuse
networking with notworking!

Who is that gorgeous networking blond? Oh it's Steve Edge, next to Audra!

The RLI MIX Team, Sue was on another planet this day, or was it Dubai?

Networking - For netting your work!

So how do we get our business? All businesses need to provide something that someone else wants, and in order to let the people who need that something know that we have it, we must let them know we have it – simple, eh?

We have decided that the one thing that works for us, and costs very little, is word of mouth marketing; this is also known as the most powerful marketing method around. Besides, any new business does not usually have the money for big marketing campaigns. So word of mouth it is and the best way to spread the word is to talk to people - people who either want it themselves, or know someone else who does - this is why we **network, network, network!**

We get the majority of our business from networking, which includes keeping in touch with contacts from our previous lives in our respective industries.

By no means is it easy, you have to talk to people, you have to go to places and you have to keep in contact with people. Audra remembers feeling low during a poor spell and she just hid away, lying on her sofa for nearly three weeks, until a friend kicked her up the bottom and told her to get networking again.

Why not do it yourself?

It paid off so well that we decided to form our own networking group in London called The RLI MIX in 2007 with business associates Terry Cole who is a business development guru, Steve Edge, a one of a kind designer who you have to see to believe and Jayne Rafter. Jayne is the editor of the RLI magazine, the world's only global retail and leisure magazine. Jointly we decided to invite our key clients, about 100 or so, to our first networking event in a wine bar in London.

We only invited key business influencers and decision-makers such as Partners, Managing Directors and Directors for example so that real business could be done. We also felt that there were few business/social events that brought together people of the same calibre and from complementary industries. We decided to hold the meetings bi-monthly in different locations in London and collectively we set about making it a success. The first event had over 80 people, it was a success and the word soon spread and now, after two years, we have to limit the numbers as typically 150 people want to come each time, fantastic eh? We even held a Xmas RLI MIX on a yacht, up the Thames! Companies that were attending then began to ask if they could sponsor events, which obviously lifts their profile, so now each event is sponsored and the sponsors bring along brochures, put up a stand and it works wonderfully. Each event gets published in the RLI magazine globally which, in turn, enables foreign visitors to attend the events; we even had Hollywood architects turn up last year, which gave us a great buzz.

So our RLI Mix is now highly successful and always fun where many relationships are formed and business projects undertaken. Read about the events yourself at **www.rli.uk.com.** These events have also been a great platform to let people know what we are up to; for example, when we set up the Dubai office, we had lots of interest and this has allowed us to form partnerships and also to find out what complementary services we can gain from joint ventures and alliances.

Oh the power of it all!

We attend all sorts of networking events, and one group that we joined was Business Network International (BNI) in our respective hometowns. For Sue it was very successful as we landed an MOD project among others in a very specialist area for over a year. We also met our printer who prints our manuals and business literature and we made lots of new friends as well. However, Audra's smaller town chapter was not quite as successful although indirectly we did meet our first LLP (Limited Liability Partnership) partner through an introduction, so it was worth it. The fact is you never know till you go and you'll get nothing by not attending in the first place, so go!!!

Here is a nice story actually associated with BNI which shows how Sue found out that BNI even existed and then how she joined. Sue had signed up with Ecademy, an online business networking forum; Audra didn't as she is not so keen on anything that involves technology! There was a networking event advertised that was being hosted by Ecademy in a nice bar on the waterfront so off she went, any excuse to walk into a bar alone! Sue particularly likes these events as they are normally held in wine bars and there are normally loads more men than women so, as a single woman, it is an easy way to go to a bar alone and just see who might be there!

So Sue went off to the networking event hosted in Bristol and met two people who have been instrumental in her life ever since. Despite the fact that during the event a man who shall remain nameless was giving a very boring talk – Yawn! Sue wanted to spend the time talking to everyone there, isn't that the purpose of a networking event? Not listening to someone rabbiting on, so when this nameless man said "The probable average age of everyone here is 45 and they've been married for over 15-20 years," Sue piped up with: "Can I add up all my marriages to get to that?" which was met with a stony silence!! So she slipped away to the bar!

At the bar she met a lovely lady called Blaire Palmer who, in turn, introduced her to the BNI concept and invited her to a meeting as her guest. She thought Sue would fit right in – so Sue's earlier quip had not put her off her but had warmed her to Sue. In all seriousness, one of the benefits of having your own business is that you can be yourself, you do not have to stand on ceremony or be under the constant threat of being sacked and you have the choice to work with people you like as well as with like-minded people. You may have gathered from what you have read so far that neither Audra nor Sue is a one for being told what to do!

So if you want to be yourself and often find yourself as a square peg in a round hole then what is it you are waiting for?

Friends, beer festivals and hips!

BNI is a great platform for learning how to promote your business, including how to sum it up in 60 seconds which is a useful skill! It also brought them into contact with many people useful to the business as well as many friends. In fact, if it wasn't for BNI Sue would never have attended her first rave or beer festival – thanks Jay! Jay was a fellow BNI member who works with structural integration, a method of realigning the body, he did a great job on my hips….oh er missus! No, in all seriousness he has a wonderful skill and talent, and managed to realign Sue's hips, which had been out of line ever since her son's birth 15 years ago! Yeah, blame it on the child Sue!

So networking has many, many advantages in addition to business!

We attend various networking events at times but choose carefully what to attend, but we have to say, **no networking, no business**. It's great to take your clients to other people's events too, you know!

Sue did a presentation at BNI once on the power of networking and drew a map of how she ended up at BNI – here it is!

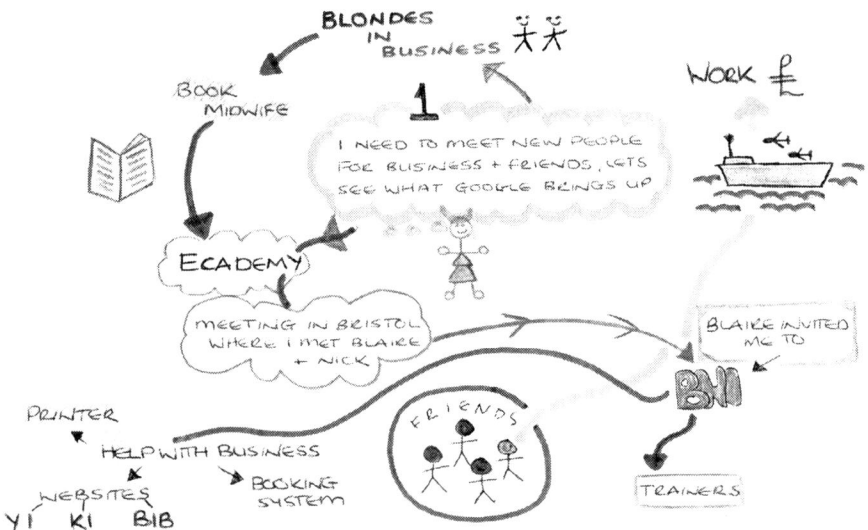

It's important to remember that networking is not always a business event. We network all the time without realising it through our friends, family and people we might meet quite randomly. If you have ever been involved in banking, insurance, multi-level marketing for example, the first thing you do is list everyone you know and then approach them to ask them who do they know who might be interested in what you do. If you go to **www.blondesinbusiness.com/networkingtool.html** you will find some useful templates to help you do this. In fact we designed a networking course for our clients, as many did not realise how to utilise their skills in business. They do now!

Remember we told you that we met through a friend in Barbados? Well, Sue's friend was friends with Audra's mum, so what friends of yours have Mums, Dads, daughters, brothers and sisters and so on and so forth who may be interested in what you do or know people who might be? We understand that asking our nearest and dearest can sometimes be harder than approaching a virtual stranger, but equally they are going to want to help you succeed more than anyone.

The internet is also a fantastic place to network, there are many good sites, such as LinkedIn, Ecademy etc., so why not research such sites, sign up and give it a go? As with anything, it does take time and it does take effort, so there's no point in signing up if you don't make the time to take part.

An example of how internet networking benefited us is Ecademy. Sue joined up and found a group that was based in Bristol run by a man called Nick Ingram; he hosted physical meetings once a month. Sue attended just a few and met two of our trainers, one of whom fulfilled the training role that we then won through attending BNI, so it was a win-win situation and all done through networking.

The thing about networking which is absolutely key is keeping in touch, following up, and helping others – the BNI philosophy is **'Givers Gain':** when someone helps you, you want to help them.

Only this morning, we have an example of just that. Sue went out to dinner with a lady called Linda whom Audra met at the British Woman's Association in Dubai and while we were talking she mentioned that it might be an idea to get on to the radio as part of our marketing strategy. She then called this morning and said that she had been listening to the radio and a gentleman was being interviewed about the benefits of training, in particular during a recession. She gave me the gentleman's name, the radio station and presenter's name. Sue now wants to help her as she is actively looking for opportunities for us.

What goes around comes around

If people know you and like you and you have helped them, they then focus on looking at ways in which to help you. I guess it also uses the principle of 'what goes around comes around' – don't focus just on results, focus on activity.

Keeping in touch is vital. Years ago Sue had a client for whom she had done some work, they got on well and became friends. Sue then left for Barbados and during that time they stayed in touch. When Sue came back to the UK, the same client had now moved to the world's largest IT software company and he introduced Sue to a manager who needed training for his department, recommended us, and we won a small pilot project. This has resulted in training over 1,000 people in 15 countries as well as other projects - all very successful and now this company is responsible for 20% of our turnover!

MIPIM – Can't remember what this stands for but everyone wants to go!

Audra attends MIPIM, which is a property festival held in Cannes each year. Up to 40,000 delegates attend and it's right in between the Cannes Film Festival and the Cannes Porn Festival, so you gotta get the right week!

Audra has always come back with projects as few, if any, training companies attend, but as we specialise in construction, engineering, design and generally Corporate Training and Development and those people attend, it's a good investment but it has to be worked out well in advance. Typically the tickets are £1,000 plus inflated accommodation and flight fees because it's a week-long event plus those other, smaller events that happen before and after! Then you have your living costs and nothing is cheap in Cannes!

Audra always has fun at these events and she works night and day, the festival hall and yachts by day and hotels, cocktail parties and yachts by night (sounds terrible!) but talking to people, introducing them to clients and remembering names, job roles and what people need is a skill. When Audra networks for our clients she has to remember all these things and more. Audra writes details gleaned from clients all over their business cards so she remembers the conversations as she comes back with hundreds of cards sometimes!

Piano rendition......when lying can work!

Audra particularly excelled herself at the famous Carlton Hotel, where she took her clients for a champagne reception and blatantly lied to her guests by telling them she could play the piano. There happened to be a baby grand in the foyer and to Audra's horror a client asked her to do a duet with him as he was a classical fan and she had already mentioned her favourite as being Handel's *Water Music*! Looking very glam in her long black gown, she edged to the piano with the dapper male, who held the seat open for her while she placed her shaky touché on it and cracked her fingers in anticipation of delivering a fabulous rendition of.........Les Dawson's crappy concerto! Only Brits will know Les Dawson who played all the right notes but not necessarily in the right order!!!

However, the client started to play properly and Audra just moved forward and back and swayed accordingly in time to the music... she was sussed by the client who laughed and carried on while she played up.... but he was eventually asked to leave as they thought Audra was the pianist and then the game was up and her tribute to Les Dawson ensued! Needless to say, there was laughter and Audra made a lot of friends that night... now let me see, what did she gain from that trip? Oh yes, a great client actually, The RPA Group, who then went on to hire our services and sponsor our networking group the RLI MIX. So you see, even when you have fun, and especially when you have fun, you can gain clients.

Who are you sitting next to?

Another example of networking that happened only this week. Coming home on the plane from Dubai, Sue was asked to move seats for the take-off and found herself sitting next to a really nice man who had recently taken up a job in Dubai. During the time they were sitting next to one another, they had the usual conversation of "What do you do?" and he asked for Sue's card as he was looking for a training company as part of his new role!

So here are our recommended Networking tips:

- Find out what networking events are going on in your area

- Join some online networking forums

- Always have your business cards to hand (Sue was VERY bad at this – but is now improving!)

- Talk to people, initiate a conversation with the person sat next to you on the plane; even if it doesn't result in business it might make the journey a damn sight more interesting and might result in a new friendship!

  (Quick warning here if you are a woman: men sometimes pretend they are interested in doing business with you, when actually they have very different ideas! We can confirm that this happens to brunettes and red-heads as well as blondes!)

- One last tip, one should never get drunk at such events, but we must admit we have both fallen off the wagon at some point! It has to be said we're good girls 99% of the time!

Remember, Networking Works - **if** you put in the effort and keep in contact and give as well as receive. Give it a go – what have you to lose?

GOALS AND VALUES

Aim – Fire!

Blue paint, wet knickers and a free beer!

So what on earth do those three things have to do with Goals and Values?

Let us tell you...

Although we spend a great deal of time talking to one another, we rarely see each other, probably only about four times year sadly, we couldn't live further apart if we had planned it – South East to South West.

One of the most amazing things that we discovered was that we both had always written down our goals.

So when we decided that we were going to go into business together we agreed to write down our personal goals for the business and ourselves separately and then compare notes. We couldn't believe just how similar they were! We were so chuffed at this as it gave us confidence that we both wanted the same things. In 2008 Audra also wrote a letter to Mother Goddess, she read it out to Sue over the phone and then sealed it in an envelope and said we would open it in 2009 and see how we did.

Sue has always gone on and on about how she loves New Year in Barbados. They actually call it Old Year's Night there – a little piece of useless information for you!

She loves the party in First Street and then going down to the beach with everyone and watching the fireworks from all the surrounding hotels, and she always has the same thought each New Year 'I wonder what this year will bring?'

So Audra, being the wonderful friend that she is and also the more organised and money-savvy one of the two, arranged for them to spend Old Year's Night 2008 in Barbados. However, sadly Audra didn't make it! We landed on the 30th December and had our first day on the beach on New Year's Eve. By 2 p.m. Audra was so sick, due either to a bug or drinking too many rum punches on the beach, that she missed the party on the beach that night. This is probably one of the only things we will never agree on: was it a bug or over-indulgence? But suffice it to say, Sue has never heard of a bug that makes you lose your memory temporarily!

We said that we would open the letter to Mother Goddess and read our goals at Sue's most favourite place in the whole wide world (currently!), North Point. So we hired a car and went off for the day all excited and Audra fully recovered, with the letter and goals all tucked away in our beach bag. It was a beautiful sunny day, not a cloud in the sky and we felt like Thelma and Louise on tour.

Eventually, navigating our way across very bumpy narrow tracks, we arrived. We parked the car which, by now, we had discovered had no suspension, and with our sore bums, we clambered over the rocks to get to the little seat with the hessian roof on the cliff edge. Quite a terrifying experience with two blonde accident-prone women!

Before we sat down we saw a sign on a pole saying 'wet paint' but didn't take much notice and sat down. We opened our letter to Mother Goddess and Audra was hanging on to it with dear life as well as trying to read it out loud, when a man came along, cigarette hanging out of his mouth and started to take down the wet paint sign; we looked at him and smiled through clenched teeth - we were trying to have a spiritual and profound moment here!

Once he left, Audra continued reading, and we were so pleased because 90% of what we had requested and desired had come true. So we then started to write our business goals for 2010, which is when Sue suggested that a beer might make the whole process easier as it might help us to be more creative.

So Audra went to stand up and couldn't. She started wailing, "I'm stuck, I'm stuck." Sue became completely hysterical at this point, realising that they had sat on a freshly-painted bench. Audra was screaming, tearing her flesh from the bench and was shouting "Look, look." Sue could not look at Audra, she was in so much fear of embarrassing herself; she kept saying "Stop it, stop it, you'll make me have an accident!" (three kids, what do you expect?)

Sue eventually managed to get a grip of herself and her bladder and looked at Audra - and this is what she saw!

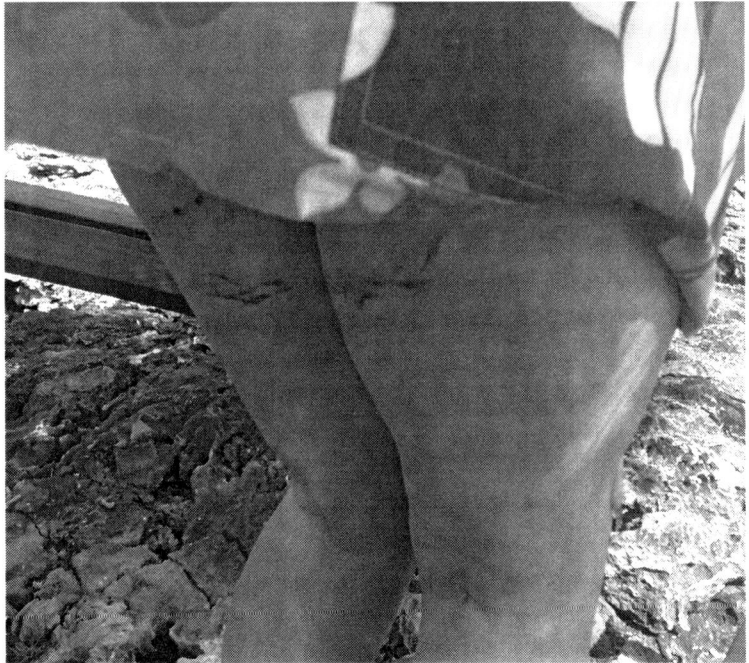

Audra hadn't wanted to mention whose legs these were, but as she insisted on the picture of Sue's messy house, it seems only fair!

We eventually managed to make our way to the bar, giggling and laughing and generally getting ourselves noticed, when the bar man, who was also the same man who had removed the wet paint sign, asked us if we were okay, and we duly showed him our bums! He graciously gave us free beers and joined in our laughter, pleased that we weren't going to sue him! We sat down next to two guys and a woman. One of the guys we decided looked like Nicholas Cage, he had a big hat on and sunglasses, so we were quite excited as he was the single one of the three! We then asked him to remove his hat and glasses and, how can we put this politely, ummmm, it was a BIG disappointment – keep up the disguise, Russ! We then told them the wet paint story and became firm friends over a few more beers and ended up seeing them most nights at our favourite end-of-the-day beach bar, Surfside.

So what has this got to do with goals? Not a lot really but it's a great story eh?!

But seriously, writing down your goals works, it really does. There a loads of theories as to why it works but, quite frankly, we are not really interested, it works and that's that!

Here is an excerpt from Sue's journal that shows how writing things down really works!

Friday 2nd July 2004

How wonderful to have an insight so early in the day and one that is going to have a MASSIVE impact, that is the second time Impact has shown itself to me, I believe, no, I think it should be a brand name – for either the training or the series of seminars – training that has a REAL return on investment.

And as for values, it is so important that whoever you work with has similar values to yourself, whether that is a partner, a colleague, a company etc. If your values do not align then there is trouble ahead, guaranteed.

Also having values that you have thought about really can help when you have to make tough decisions. Knowing what in your heart of hearts is right for you and what you believe in gives you guidance when you most need it. The trouble with life is that it throws you curve balls, and when those balls hit you, you are often so stunned you can't think straight, so knowing your values and standards can really help. We suggest you write these down too, you may need to refer to them when the going gets really tough!

The reason we put the two together, Goals and Values, is simply this: You may have a goal to be a multi millionaire – what would you do to achieve that? Rob a bank, con old ladies? If you don't hold any value in honesty, laws, and the older generation then, yes, that might be the route you take!

Knowing your values is equally important in your day-to-day work. You may, like us, have made the mistake of letting work take over your life. You may have forgotten WHY you work, if it's to provide for your family or to retire young, or whatever, you may not have a family at the end of it and you may not have time to enjoy your retirement if you have abused your families and your body through neglect.

Having a work/life balance is a choice and we strongly urge you to make the right choice!

In 1995 Sue had the wake-up call of her life. She had three young children and a husband and been working solidly for a training company; she never ever stopped and was travelling about 40,000 miles a year. She also played hard as well as worked hard! One morning she woke up at her friend's house with what felt like a really bad cold, yet she still went to work. When she arrived she felt very ill, she wanted to go home but felt too ill to drive. Her husband came and collected her, and she doesn't remember any more. She ended up in a coma in hospital suffering from viral encephalitis, which is life threatening, and was told it was stress-related. When the body is worn out, a simple cold can have an almighty impact and with immune defences low, the simple cold virus can travel to many parts of the body and wreak havoc. Sue had three months off work to recover and the headaches lasted for a further two years.

That experience has never left her and has had a huge impact on her decisions about her work/life balance ever since. Please, Please, Please listen to this and don't let work dominate your life to the extent that it threatens it!

Of course hard work is necessary, of course long hours may be required, but be aware that you need rest, you need sleep, you need nights out to let your hair down, you need 'ME time'. Don't feel guilty for needing it or wanting it either – you deserve it – especially the nights out!

So keep the goal in mind, and ensure that the journey that you take to get to that goal is a road travelled that you are proud of. There are many rich and lonely people out there. Money does not make you happy; it really, really does not. Yes, it makes life easier in many, many ways and you can have both, but in order to have both you need to plan how and why you are going to do it and remind yourself of both your goals and your values on at least an annual basis.

Having said all of that, sometimes opportunities come along that aren't planned, so then what do you do? More often than not, we say YES! Many people have said to us that we are lucky, but we know it is often because we say YES – that should be the default answer! Many people say we have exciting lives and always a story to tell – well, one thing we can say is if you always say no, then you will never ever have a story to tell, and that is for sure – so start saying YES and see what stories you come up with.

We've just had a thought! What about meeting us in Barbados and sitting and reading our goals together? Say YES, give us a call, sounds like a plan Stan!

Tips and tools

- Write down your goals

- Work out your values

- Get some exercises that will help you from our website

- Manage your work/life balance

- Keep healthy – only smoke light cigarettes and drink light beer!

- Meet Sue and Audra in Barbados for New Year every year!

POSITIVES AND NEGATIVES

We're not talking batteries!

Positive Thinking! Support teams left right and centre!

UK team

We are pretty much on our own in terms of running the companies and some of you will be totally alone, but remember this: Audra built up her first company over six years totally alone and through a mini-recession, divorce and bereavement, and Sue has brought up her three children pretty much alone on and off and often in very difficult circumstances. So we know what can be done and that you might also have challenging challenges, or a deep pile of poo to wade through – you are not alone!

But whether you have a business partner or not it's good to find a support network, professional or personal; find people who are positive and want you to succeed.

They may be totally unrelated to you, which is a good thing as they are unbiased and objective, but always able to give good advice. Look out for these people and use them! It's great to be their support arm in return, 'Givers gain' as Ivan Misner of BNI (Business Network International) says!

We always try to stay positive or we force ourselves to get in a positive frame of mind! Especially when faced with a challenge, issue or situation, we psyche ourselves up for it when we can. But some situations are out of our control, let's take the current recession. We didn't plan to write a book at this time, but maybe it was the right time?

If we can help more people to start a business during a time of uncertainty, as opposed to a buoyant time, than this is a perfect time to release the book. We didn't plan to launch a company in Dubai in September 2008 (beginning of a global recession!) but maybe it was the right time; it's enabled us to re-strategise, understand the market better and deliver a service that our clients need rather than desire. Collaboration has been the lesson learned in Dubai and we have a great team in Dubai all working towards giving other members business through sharing clients. That would not have happened if our operation in Dubai was not implemented.

Ex-pat Dubai!

Ahh, thank God for the ex-pats! Sounds like a film title and it will be, believe us! What a combination of mad, fabulous and interesting characters there are in Dubai! We fit right in! It's so amusing to see all the cultures working together, but the best thing of all has been the support and goodwill of people wanting to make a success of it out there. Not people who want to rush in, cream as much cash as they can and get out; we mean the real long-term, business-creating people who want to make a difference and want to make Dubai their home. They have already made sacrifices, such as leaving families and pets at home (the pet sacrifice is the only thing that concerned us but we're sorting that out!).

We have met people before going to Dubai and then again by chance in Dubai (which happens a lot, it's not a coincidence, and it's meant to happen that way). We have also met some phenomenal people who have become just as good friends as long-term UK buddies.

Our friends in Dubai

Tom Miles regularly puts us up for free just to help us get started... and the fact that he is mentioned in the book is a debt repaid, okay Tom? Tom is an all-American, party-loving, friendly guy who has a great network of friends who have all became friends of ours and they have been very supportive business-wise too. This friendship led us to gaining business with his company and we have helped his team gain promotions through leadership training, so pat on the back for all!

Rachel Walton, a networking buddy of Audra's, guided us in the past two years around Dubai with introductions and free lodgings; again, anything to help and Rachel and the girlie network regularly put work each others' way, with no money involved, as it's great doing a favour and more work has come that way. It does help that Rachel is a 6 foot 2 ex-model who is stunning and can get an invitation to anywhere while we have been more used to sliding in under the radar! In the early days, of course!

Clients too have become friends over the years and a magnificent support team in many instances. Jamshid Soheili is an Engineering Director who has hired our services over the years and always introduced us outside his circle as he believed in the work we delivered and loved our style.

Dealing with negativity –
you can't tell them to bugger off, or can you?

This can be caused by jealousy or envy and generally families and friends are guilty of this, but it can come from a place of worry and good intention!

Questions like "Do you think you should be going to Dubai now?" (recession time). Sensible enough but not what you really need to hear as you leave for the airport, is it? No, it doesn't help, but it came from good intent.

Sam (Sue's son) really believed in Sue from a very young age and happily told a family member that Mummy would be a millionaire one day and that family member laughed. It hurt Sue and Sam, but comments like that just make them more determined. You will deal with doubts from time to time but always keep focussed. Try to recognise what people mean by their comments, what do you think their internal dialogue is like? How different from them are you and your internal dialogue? People do say things out of love, too, remember and they may not want you changing yourself or leaving the country, town or house! People have limited beliefs about themselves and others and none of this is based on reality and you have to keep your belief in yourself going so cast those comments off and **MOVE ON!**

Support yourself - what about your negativity?

What do you say to yourself on a constant basis? Do you have stock, standard responses to negative situations? So beware of your own negativity, as it festers and bores the pants off everyone else! Three years ago, Audra had this amazing 16-week cold or something ridiculous and always started a conversation to Sue with how many days and then weeks it had lasted! Sue, with her annoying behaviour-corrective skill, said "Audra, don't you think it might go away if you stop talking about it and making it the biggest thing on your list? Stop thinking and talking about it and it will go away!" And she was right, it went away as it wasn't important.

It had lingered through constant discussion. But it really taught Audra to concentrate on positive things when alone with her thoughts, as you need to rely on yourself as well as others, right? So if you have a cold, we don't want to hear about it, it's not big and it's not clever (but if you have a cold that lasts longer than 16 weeks Audra would really like to hear from you and compare notes!).

Things you can do to combat negativity!

Okay, so you can't tell them to bugger off, but there are little things that can put you in the right frame of mind. For example, affirmations may work for you... we see them everywhere and they make us feel energised and positive, like:

- It's all happening perfectly

- You are where you are meant to be on your journey

- All lessons are a journey that you must make to become better

- If you're running with the ball you're going to get tackled – Audra struggles with this one, maybe because she has sport phobia and is slightly dyslexic! (Did we tell you about the time she wrote to Dear Satan at Christmas time?)

- Aim high and you'll always get more than you would if you aimed low

We use these and borrow others from time to time!

Give yourself a pep talk before you venture into any and every conversation or sales pitch. Visualise what you want the outcome to be and don't panic if the outcome is not what you wanted it to be! Just get into the habit of thinking positively and your behaviour will automatically become positive in any given situation.

Lists and books!!!

Women are fab at lists; we blondies even have lists of the lists we have made!

We have to list...wonderful!!! Until you come to cross things off and you fall into a coma! So be realistic, list a few things and if there are too many make separate lists for separate days and don't look at them till that day arrives! You'll be amazed at what you can achieve and there's nothing better than crossing off things to do from the next day's list...oh what bliss!!!!! We know how to live, eh?

Books, books and more books! We have already mentioned Audra's limited attention span, so reading whole books is a challenge unless they are the size of postage stamps! So if you are not a reader, buy CDs of the books, films of the books, do whatever you need to do – but it's important to fill your brain with new ways of thinking, to always be learning something new!

But listen, when you are feeling really low and just don't want to do any of it...JUST DO SOMETHING! Action gets you where you want to be, know that, take it on board and live it!

No sugar, thank you!

Generally, we have an 'I'll show you' attitude! To be honest we have both had our fair share of being called 'dumb blondes' and know how to use it to our advantage! Audra gets her whole house and garden chores done through being a dumb blonde! Suckers!!! Remarks like 'dumb blonde' have never fazed us.

So take this situation. A boardroom full of men and then there is Audra. She is the only female in the room of ten men folk and is blonde to boot.

"I'll have a tea with one sugar please...." piped up the CEO of an astronomically-large global organisation... and with that Audra looked around the room and stared right back at him and said "That's nice, (smiled sweetly) I'll have mine without thank you!" An apology ensued with the offering of an Earl Grey! Ta very much Gov'ner!

Bollywood blonde

Audra remembers a particular day when Rachel and she were in Dubai (Rachel the model who, by the way, wants to be an honorary blonde, along with some chaps we may add!) - anyway, where were we? Oh yes, they went the wrong way to Abu Dhabi, through the most horrendous traffic jam, and those of you who have been in traffic at 9 a.m. in Dubai will understand what a nightmare that is - and it brought them back to where they started an hour earlier! They made it, an hour late, to the clients, who then could not see them for long and had had a bad day themselves, and then their next appointments were cancelled, so back to Dubai they went.

En route (apart from being followed by a local in his full headdress, beckoning them to call him, though quite how they could they didn't know!) Audra was contacted by a very important client to say that they could not see her that trip at all and all the training she had planned had been shelved! Disaster, recession in the UK and Dubai, Audra felt like she was being hit from all sides that day! They made for the last meeting of the day, banging their heads on the dashboard and made for a rather beautiful terrace called the Vista Bar, which is in the Intercontinental Hotel Dubai Festival City… always a fabulous drinking spot with gorgeous food and a beautiful sunset to boot. How lovely it would have been if it were a successful day! But although it wasn't a successful day they did end up in a scene of Bollywood 'paps', directors, film stars and autograph hunters! How did that happen?!

Rachel and Audra sat down and looked at each other as if to say 'Why do we bother?' Then they listed all the benefits of being self-employed, being in control and how they could work their way through this by helping each other and believing in each other too… so they gave themselves a pat on the back, glugged back the Marlborough County and began to notice a lot of activity. They were smack bang in the middle of a press conference for a Bollywood movie called Delhi 6! They laughed and said loudly "No pictures please, we want our privacy!" And with that, one of the photographers turned and started to take pictures of them! Believing in her hype, Audra then went on to tell him that they were also movie stars and had just finished a movie called London 5…(that's all that came to mind once he mentioned Delhi 6, sorry!) Rachel laughed and he asked them for their credentials! The girls showed their very non-Bollywood business cards and he laughed some more and then told the girls that half of the population of India would cut off their right arm to be sat where they were, next to the hero and heroine of the movie and the director! We couldn't tell you their names for toffee, but everyone in Dubai knew of them!

They left, having had some photos taken and having mingled with stars (or so they say!), slightly tipsy but completely motivated even though it hadn't been a successful day. You never know what's around the corner and it's not all business, so enjoy every moment, it could end up in a book!

Tips! Here's what works for us!

- The right frame of mind will set you on the right road when things get scary

- Go in knowing you are going to win – manage your expectations

- List by the bed! Personal and professional list (mind you, our men have not appeared yet, but perfection does take time I understand!)

- Surround yourself with positive people

- Affirmations – put them where you can see them each day, maybe on bright yellow cards for example

- Talk to someone positive

- Get practical advice

- Remember, family and friends can be the largest support network you have and the biggest critiques so keep them and yourself in check, please

- Don't let people redirect you or steal your dream, keep working towards it and for your own reasons

- Prove the buggers wrong!

- DO IT!

And remember, it's all happening perfectly!

LIGHTS, CAMERA, ACTION!

Go for it!

Itchy crotches, money and goodbye!

So now for the all-important chapter. You may be reading this one first and, if that is so, then congratulations for wanting to take immediate action, but please do read the rest of the book as (even if we do say so ourselves) it has a few gems that just might be useful too!

We have a little story about **'you don't know what you don't know'**. Think about it!

We do a lot of presentation-skills training, and for this one particular course we were working together. We can't give too much detail as we don't want to give away the name of the client, but it was early morning, we were getting ready to set up in the boardroom, we were surrounded by pictures of previous heads of the company in black and white photographs and the room was rather warm to say the least. Audra piped up that she didn't feel too good, and the next thing she was on the floor – she had fainted!

Sue was so scared, for three reasons: she didn't fancy giving Audra the kiss of life!; she didn't want to run the course alone; and, thirdly, about poor Audra!! In that order! Suffice it to say, Audra recovered with lots of water, open windows and fussing. Sue got her through the day, plus had some major laughs. Audra has a horrid affliction, nothing that can be transmitted fortunately, but she can't sleep the night before she runs a course, even if she has done it a thousand times, bless her. No doubt this was a contributor to the fainting!

It's a guy thing!

On the very same day, one of the guys presenting had a little habit that he wasn't aware of, but everyone else in the room was, you couldn't miss it! He kept rubbing his genitals while presenting! Well, Audra and Sue just couldn't look at each other, but fortunately one of his workmates started laughing, so we all could – it was so funny! He didn't understand till Audra showed him the footage back, as we film this course. Not many people would be brave enough in real life to tell someone about such a habit...we would, but we let the film do it for us in this instance.... and the result? Instant cure, but he needed to be told - feedback is great, isn't it?

So what do you do - or not do? What do you know - or not know? Ask, observe and review yourself and be ready for whatever the feedback might be!

This might seem a strange thing to start an action-planning chapter off with, but we wanted to have a laugh! But seriously, we really do believe that it is essential that you do a job that you are naturally good at, one that you love and one that you are happy to put your heart and soul into.

- So what are you good at?

- What do you love doing?

- What do others think you are good at?

- Are you brave enough to accept honest feedback?

- Are you humble enough to accept honest feedback?

That's a toughie!

- What skills do you have?

- What skills don't you have?

Action planning and summary check-list

Let's start with a basic check-list of things that we think a business needs to survive:

- A defined product or service

- Customers – that would help!

- Financial help – that would be nice but not necessary

- Marketing

- Business planning

- A strategy

There are so many things to think about and you do need to think about them!

We all know planning is a must, which it is, but so is doing! So we have come up with a whole host of questions that you can ask yourself, and your support network, which will then, hopefully, give you an idea on areas that you either need training in and/or where you will need outside help and guidance. We have also provided a list of resources that may be useful when looking for additional help.

Be the best that you can be!

So your product or service:

- Is this something that you can do personally or do you need outside help?

- Where will you get additional help? If you don't need it now, you will as you grow (think positive!)

- How will you know that this help is reliable and provides an excellent service?

- Will you need contracts? Do you know how to write a contract?

- Do you need to patent your product?

- What is your competition? Do you know who they are? Do you know how to research them?

- What makes you different? What will make you different – be specific!

Resources

www.businesslink.gov.uk

www.ehow.com/about_4571513_patenting-an-idea. html

www.yourimpact.co.uk

The customer is always right!

- Who are likely to be your customers?

- Why?

- What do they want that they can't already get easily?

- What are the industries you should focus on in particular, if any?

- What do you know about these industries?

- Are there events that you can attend that would suit your offering?

- Where else will you find these customers?

- What suitable networking events can you attend?

- Do you want to buy lists? Where from – are they good – can someone recommend?

- Current contacts?

- Your circle of friends, family, acquaintances?

Resources

www.blondesinbusiness.com/usefulinfo.htm

www.bni.com

www.referralinstitute.com

Money, money, money!

Ah yes, money – we are guessing that this is one of the reasons you want to have your own business or be the best in your current employment. Now, we certainly don't want to put you off immediately, but if you think that having your own business instantly makes you rich, you can forget that notion immediately! Strangely enough, some people think that if you have your own business you must be rich and we are sure you will be, but not at first. In fact, you are more likely to have less money than ever before in the first few years. What you have to remember is that your money, your salary in fact, is from profit only, which is after expenses, running costs, tax, VAT etc. If there is money left after that, then you can have some! Have you ever watched *Dragons' Den*? (You may have realised this is Sue's favourite programme and that the odd mention may get her an invitation to the show!). One of the questions that is often asked is 'What do you intend to spend the money on?' and often people include wages in their long shopping list which is always frowned upon by the Dragons! Can you see why, as investors, this may displease them?

So make a list of ALL the costs associated with your product or service, and don't forget the cost of the sale! Travel expenses, meals, coffee, marketing materials (one of the great things about being green and about technology is that these costs can be drastically reduced compared to what they used to be) and then also add 15% for the unthought-of things! The unexpected expenses such as one of Sue's foster dogs, Rusty, cost her £120.00 in February 2009 when he ate through two cables which meant she had to buy a new laptop lead (£40.00) and a new printer (£80.00)! Those were unexpected costs!

Now, chin up, it's not all bad, but it is good to face the facts — over 90% of new businesses fail in the first two years and it is our belief that this is because these things have not been considered properly.

Even if you have had a business loan to help you out initially, it needs to be paid back one way or another. So keep costs down, borrow the minimum if any at all and do get reliable help and advice that can be trusted completely.

Ahhhhh....it's The End!

Thank you for reading our book, we hope you got a lot from it and even laughed along the way. We certainly laughed while we were writing it and have so much material left over there's enough for another book...oh no!!!!! So you may be seeing us on the shelves again soon, until then feel the fear and go for it. Thoughts become things remember, and always remain positive, and if things aren't happening the way you had planned, well maybe it's really happening perfectly, you just don't see it that way....yet!

Blondes in Business signing off

XX

PS watch out for the next book!

Lightning Source UK Ltd
Milton Keynes UK
21 August 2009

142923UK00001B/2/P